Today with

CW00740253

Today with Ezekiel

Volume Two

Clifford Hill

British Library Cataloguing in Publication Data:
a catalogue record for this publication
is available from the British Library

ISBN   978-1-912052-87-5

The right of Clifford Hill to be identified
as the author of this work has been asserted by him
in accordance with the Copyright, Designs and Patents Act 1988

Typeset in 10.5pt Minion Pro at Haddington, Scotland

Printed by Bell and Bain, Glasgow

Cover image by Anthony Whelan

CONTENTS

INTRODUCTION TO THE '*TODAY*' SERIES

Through the prophets of ancient Israel, God released into the world a unique revelation of his nature and purposes. The record of the ministry of the prophets that we have from Isaiah to Malachi is a priceless treasure trove of spiritual truth. It is of immense value for all those who wish to go deeper in their knowledge and understanding of God.

The prophets were keen observers of the social environment, and they kept a watchful eye on the international situation as well as the domestic scene. In order to understand their message, it is essential to have a good knowledge of the historical background to each of their ministries. Without such an understanding, their work and their words remain obscure.

Each of the prophets had a close walk with God through which they were able to bring his word to their generation. In this series we are seeking to provide an understanding of their world and their experience of God, which is used to unlock the barriers of language and culture so that the word of God comes alive and fresh.

Today with Ezekiel, like each of the books in the '*Today*' series, is not a 'commentary' in the technical sense of that word: it is a series of studies to make reading the prophets a pleasurable and rewarding exercise. It covers the whole Book of Ezekiel explaining the background and meaning behind the Hebrew text to bring its message alive. We have tried to avoid technical language and to open up the text to the ordinary reader in an endeavour to discover the life and ministry of this great servant of God.

SHORT INTRODUCTION TO THE BOOK OF EZEKIEL

The Introduction to Volume 1 covered the general structure of the Book of Ezekiel, the man, and his message. We are repeating some of that here, but we are not including the historical setting to the Book of Ezekiel which is extremely important for an understanding of the message. That is in the Introduction to Volume 1 which should be read before embarking on Volume 2.

It is advisable to have an open Bible at the same time as reading this book because the Scripture quoted at the beginning of each study is only a small part of the text that is being studied.

Structure of Ezekiel

The Book of Ezekiel is unique among the prophets of Israel both in terms of its message and its historical background. Without a thorough knowledge of the latter its message would be meaningless. The book is a story from beginning to end, starting with a great storm through which Ezekiel is commissioned by God, and ending with a vision of the newly restored land of Israel after the end of the exile. The story is told by Ezekiel to his fellow exiles in Babylon in the 6th century BC. The whole book was written in Babylon during the period 593 to 571 BC. This is the conclusion reached by many biblical scholars with the final date being that of the last dated prophecy which is in Ezekiel 29:17.

The book has four divisions each with a distinctive characteristic:

Section One: Chapters 1 – 24 contain material referring to the period before the destruction of Jerusalem in 586.[1]

Section Two: Chapters 25 – 32 are a collection of oracles against foreign nations.

Section Three: Chapters 33 – 39 are oracles relating to post-586 with their hopes of restoration.

Section Four: The final section chapters 40 – 48 sets out the hopes for the future restoration of the temple and its religious activities.

---

1 Vol. 1 covers chapters 1 – 21 while Vol. 2 covers chapter 22 on.

Chronology

A unique characteristic of the Book of Ezekiel is its chronological format which has been carefully constructed in date order. A number of dates are given and in two cases there are double dates which is because both the Hebraic and Babylonian calendars are used.

Another unique characteristic of the Book of Ezekiel is that it is entirely written in Babylon during the 12 year period 593 – 571 BC. The last dated oracle is in 24:1 which is actually 588 and was the year that Nebuchadnezzar began his two-year siege of Jerusalem. The last dated prophecy is about Nebuchadnezzar setting his long siege against Tyre which began in 588 and is recorded in Ezekiel 29:17.

Ezekiel: The Man

Very little is known about Ezekiel's early life other than the fact that his father was Buzi. He was a priest from the family of Zadok, from whom the Chief Priest was appointed, and they were the senior officials in the temple priesthood and the only ones allowed to approach the Holy of Holies and to discharge ceremonial duties on behalf of the nation. Ezekiel would have had a thorough training in the 'Book of the Law' discovered in the lifetime of Josiah thought to be part of Deuteronomy. Ezekiel is thought to have taken a copy with him when he was forced to join the company of exiles from Jerusalem. He may also have had other scrolls of the prophets, or history, or the Psalms. There is evidence that he had a copy of Jeremiah's sayings which he quotes, eg Ezekiel 13:10 and Jeremiah 6:14 where they both speak of "*peace when there is no peace*".

Family Man

We know that Ezekiel was married and that his wife was "*the delight of his eyes*" (24:16), who died at the height of his ministry. We know that he was a musician who played an instrument and that he had a beautiful singing voice and that he used to lead times of worship in his own home for the local community of believers who lived in the settlement at Tel Abib, "*My people come to you, as they usually do, and sit before you to listen to your words*" (33:31).

Leadership

We know also that Ezekiel's ministry was recognised throughout the exile population and that elders from the scattered communities used to come regularly to his home and sit at his feet for teaching and to listen to any word from the Lord that he may have received. "*Some of the elders of Israel came to me and sat down in front of me*" (14:1).

Teacher

We also know that he was regarded as a teacher of the word of God, and that he exercised a pastoral ministry dealing with many of the personal issues that were occurring amongst the settlements where people were getting into idolatrous practices, and he had to speak very firmly to the elders. "*Will you defile yourselves the way your fathers did and lust after their vile images?*" (20:30).

Prophet

Ezekiel also exercised a prophetic ministry – listening to the Lord and reporting to the elders things that he was hearing. "*The word of the Lord came to me: Son of man set your face against Jerusalem and preach against the sanctuary. Prophesy against the land . . .*" (21:1).

Visions

Ezekiel was given a number of visions beginning with one that led to his call to ministry recorded in chapter 1:1 – 3:15. This was triggered by a great storm with thunder and lightning that led to him seeing the kind of living creatures that were depicted in the Temple in Jerusalem and similar to the figures in the vision described in Isaiah 6. This was covered in volume 1.

In chapter 7 Ezekiel reached the point where God said to him that the end had come, God would no longer be patient waiting for the people of Judah to repent. Ezekiel received the message, "*Disaster! An unheard-of disaster is coming. The end has come! The end has come!*" (7:5). In the following chapter Ezekiel records the elders coming to sit before him and he then related to them a vision of what was happening in Jerusalem that occupies four chapters and is concluded at the end of chapter 11.

INTRODUCTION TO *TODAY WITH EZEKIEL* VOLUME 2

Sins of The Fathers

Ezekiel's main task in the early years of his ministry, which is covered in Volume 1, was to deal with the sense of devastation and abandonment by God among the exiles in Babylon. He had to deal with what the exiles saw as the 'injustice' of God in abandoning them to their enemies. He also had to demolish the proverbial saying, *"The fathers have eaten sour grapes and the children's teeth are set on edge" (Jer 31:29; Ezek 18:2).*

The belief among the exiles was that they were suffering in Babylon because of the sins of their fathers. Underlying this belief is the concept of 'corporate responsibility' for sin which goes right back to the giving of the Law at Mount Sinai where it is written in the Decalogue. The Second Commandment banning idolatry says, *"I the Lord your God am a jealous God, punishing the children for the sins of the fathers to the third and fourth generation of those who hate me"* (Deut 5:9). The truth behind this statement was that if the fathers worshipped idols, this would affect their children and grandchildren who would follow their example. Ezekiel had to modify this teaching by saying that each generation had the responsibility of seeking truth for themselves.

Desecrated the Sabbaths

This teaching that is embedded in chapter 20 begins with the command that Ezekiel should confront the elders with the detestable practices of their fathers, how in each generation they had rebelled against God. He said that right from the time of Moses God had said, *"Each of you, get rid of the vile images you have set your eyes on, and do not defile yourselves with the idols of Egypt"* (20:7). At that time God also said. *"I gave them my Sabbaths as a sign between us, so that they would know that I the Lord made them holy"* (20:12). But they utterly desecrated the Sabbaths and for this reason God had warned them that he would pour out his wrath upon them.

This was what was happening now and they themselves were part of the generation that had erected altars to foreign gods on every street corner in Jerusalem. They must have been aware of this because Jeremiah had described how all the family were involved in idolatry, *"The children gather wood, the fathers light the fire, and the women knead the dough and make cakes of bread for the Queen of heaven"* (Jer 7:18).

Judgement and Wrath

Volume 1 ended with the focus upon King Zedekiah who, instead of putting his trust in God, had put his trust in Egypt, and other neighbouring countries which would be disastrous, not only for him, but for Jerusalem and the whole nation of Judah. The scene was now set for the later chapters of Ezekiel.

Volume 2 begins with warnings about the sinfulness of Jerusalem where innocent blood was shed and the city was further defiled by the worship of idols. All this demonstrated the justice of God in removing his cover of protection over the land. This prepares the way for Ezekiel to tell the exiles that judgement upon city of Jerusalem is inevitable. This would come as shattering news to all of them who still believed that Jerusalem was inviolable, that no foreigner would be allowed to enter because the temple was the place where the presence of God was dwelling. Ezekiel had yet to change their whole understanding of God.

The Gentile Nations

There follows a number of oracles and prophecies about other nations, Ammon, Moab, Edom, Philistia, Tyre and Sidon, and Egypt. These seven nations are all dealt with in groups of seven that carry particular messages of comfort to the exiles. All these are prophecies of doom, foreseeing judgement upon these Gentile nations for their attitudes and actions towards the people of Israel when Jerusalem was destroyed in 586.

Ezekiel's Second Commission

It is at this point in the narrative that Ezekiel is commissioned the second time. The first time was at his call to ministry – to pronounce doom upon the old way of life in the land of Israel. This new commission was to deal with the situation post 586 BC. This is the main theme dealt with in Volume 2 that has a much happier message than Volume 1.

In his new message Ezekiel has to teach that all people are sinners. The fall of Jerusalem as recorded in chapter 33 introduces a new side of Ezekiel himself, as leader of a house group in Tel Abib, as well as the one who teaches the elders of the scattered communities of exiles around Babylonia. It is at this point that Ezekiel starts exercising his ministry as a pastor, as well as a teacher and prophet.

Pastor and Teacher

Ezekiel speaks about the tender ministry of God as a shepherd guarding his sheep and leading them to good pastures. He begins speaking about the 'covenant of peace' that God will make with his people when he will bless them and give them prosperity. He will ensure that they have better leaders than they have ever had and they will come to know God as their Sovereign Lord.

The Return to The Land

The new message now features the end of the exile and the return of the people to the land of Israel. *"The towns will be inhabited and the ruins rebuilt"* (36:10). It is at this point that Ezekiel begins his teaching about the nature and purposes of God that had, and even today have, been misunderstood by the people of Israel since the nation was formed at Mount Sinai. The central feature is that God plans to wash his people clean from the defiling nature of sin. He himself will provide an atonement and he will give them a new heart and a new spirit, but in preparation for this they have to recognise their sinfulness and repent, *"you will loathe yourselves for your sins and detestable practices"* (36:31).

The Resurrection of The Nation

This is followed by the amazing and inspiring vision of 'The Valley of Dry Bones' – the resurrection of the nation. This prepares the way for the Messianic prophecy of a new nation cleansed from sin and led by a new leader after the pattern of King David. God himself promises to be with them, *"I will put my sanctuary among them for ever"* (37:26).

The peaceful existence of the people of Israel restored in the land, does not last. Unknown nations such as Gog and Magog attack the land of Israel and it is God himself who deals with them.

New Temple and New Jerusalem

This leads to the vision of the new temple in the new Jerusalem with the presence of God and holy worship being in the centre of the city. In the same way as Ezekiel had seen the presence of the Lord depart from the temple and leave the city of Jerusalem, which was recorded in Volume 1, he now sees the glory of the Lord returning. This comes at the height of the vision for the new temple. He is told, *"Describe the temple to the people of Israel, that they may be ashamed of their sins. Let them consider the plan, and if they are ashamed of all they have done, make known to them the design of the temple"* (43:10-11).

From the new temple a river flows out through the streets of the city into the countryside and wherever it goes, it cleanses and creates new life.

The Teaching About God

A major purpose of Ezekiel was to teach the people of Israel about the nature and purposes of God. Ezekiel recognised that the people had never understood the covenant that God established with them at Mount Sinai when Moses received the Decalogue. All the prophets faced a similar problem. Jeremiah said, *"From the time your forefathers left Egypt until now, day after day, again and again I sent you my servants the prophets. But they did not listen to me or pay attention"* (Jer 7:25).

Ezekiel used every method at his disposal for teaching the elders so that they could go back to their communities and teach the people. It was essential for them to know their own God when they were surrounded by a multitude of gods of their Gentile neighbours in Babylon. Ezekiel's teaching emphasised the holiness of God, his separation from the physical world and his difference from the gods of the Gentiles who were nothing more than wood and stone.

Ezekiel was not just a teacher he was also an evangelist. He wanted to show people of other nations that the God of Israel was the 'God of Creation' who held the nations in his hands and guided their destiny. He knew that this was God's purpose in choosing the people of Israel. They were to be a *"kingdom of priests and a holy nation"* (Ex 19:6), set aside by God, through whom he would reveal himself to the world.

Many times, Ezekiel ends his oracles to the nations with the words, *"Then they will know that I am the Lord their God"*. He would be known to the world through his actions – that he was not simply the God of Israel, but the God of all the world. The return of the exiles to the land of Israel would be a sign to the Gentiles of God's power and his justice. It will also show his love in cleansing and forgiving his people and enabling them to restore the land of Judah. The new Jerusalem with the temple at its heart would be a powerful sign of the presence of God in the midst of his people.

FOREWORD TO VOLUME TWO

In Volume One of *Today with Ezekiel*, Dr Clifford Hill described how "it must have been a bitter experience for Ezekiel to have to face the truth that the warnings of Jeremiah were true. He had said that God would not defend the city unless there was repentance. This unpalatable warning was truly a word from God that was being fulfilled. His whole world was being turned upside down."

In the Foreword to Volume One, I said the parallel with the way in which our own world has been turned upside down since 2020 is clear. The quotation from Jeremiah 6:13, *"From the least to the greatest, all are greedy for gain"* also particularly resonated as I read it in the context of the changes we are witnessing in our own society. Cliff described how Ezekiel came to the understanding that Jeremiah had been right, and that tragedy would befall the city of Jerusalem which had become full of idolatry.

Ezekiel knew that although he too was part of that rebellious nation, and though certain consequences were inevitable, nonetheless God would ultimately fulfil *HIS* promises of restoration and covenant toward the remnant Israelites then captive in Babylon. Ezekiel could see the extent to which unbelief and Godlessness had penetrated the population. We today can see parallels with our own society who have also "turned their backs upon God".

I found some aspects of the Book of Ezekiel which reveal a great deal of the character and understanding of the prophet particularly encouraging. His message is relevant to this generation more than two and a half millennia later. His words remind us that we all have access to God through prayer and can learn to listen in the quietness of our own homes and as part of small groups.

Cliff has warned for almost four decades of the deserved judgement that will come upon our own nation if we do not turn back to God. As he points out, the Book of Ezekiel contains many references to the wrath of God, but he also reminds us that Ezekiel emphasises the holiness of God and that he demands a spirit of repentance and holiness of his people if they are to have close fellowship with him.

Volume Two has much good news. God himself will be a shepherd to his people, caring for the weak, finding the strays, gathering them from all the places where they have been scattered. God will wash the people clean from their sins and give them a new heart and a new Spirit (36:24-27).

Cliff describes chapter 37 as a wonderful message of national resurrection. The dry bones become filled with new life as the whole nation is raised from the dead and God brings his people up from the grave. They will not only be new people, but God will give them a king of the line of David who will be a Good Shepherd to them and God himself will establish a covenant of peace with them. He will plant his sanctuary among them and abide with his people for ever.

The climax of Ezekiel's message is the vision of the new temple, the new Jerusalem, and the new people of faith, through whom God will fulfil his purpose of revealing his nature and his ways to all the world through his servant, the people of Israel.

Before he can reveal that vision, Cliff explains that God has to deal with those who are implacably opposed to the kingdom of God, who hate Israel and are haters of God. This is what Ezekiel presents in chapters 38 and 39. This final battle will not be for Israel to fight – God himself intervenes and deals with those who cannot be changed by human endeavour.

Nick Szkiler
February 2024

ACKNOWLEDGEMENTS

I want to acknowledge the contribution to this book made by a few of our willing proofreaders who diligently went through the text marking inaccuracies in quotations and querying many things that needed my attention. Their rigorous scrutiny has been very helpful and I want to express my gratitude to Angela Isbister, Pam Smith, Jane Ghosh and Vanessa Edmonds.

I am grateful to Nick Szkiler, Chair of Issachar Ministries, for writing the Foreword to this book, and Tony Whelan for producing the book cover. I am also grateful to the trustees and staff of Issachar Ministries, especially Christopher Cobbold and Jacqueline Barber for their willingness to distribute Volumes One and Two of *Today with Ezekiel*.

Monica and I founded Issachar Ministries back in the 1980s and we are so glad to see that it is still fulfilling its mission to 'understand the times' in which we are living today. In his Foreword Nick notes the relevance for today of the message that Ezekiel brought some 2500 years ago. The problems of war, human violence and greed are still with us today, but the revelation of the nature and purposes of God that Ezekiel discovered are greatly needed today.

I want to acknowledge the enormous contribution of Monica, my wife, who has shared with me in the writing of this book. Her tireless work behind-the-scenes in research and the presentation of Ezekiel's message is immeasurable. We are also grateful to our friend of many years Dr Jock Stein of Handsel Press for his work in producing and publishing this book. It has been a pleasure working with him.

Finally, I want to acknowledge the contribution of my daughter-in-law, the Rev Alison Hill, Vicar of St Win's, Totton, Southampton. It was Ali's preaching on Ezekiel that spoke deeply to me and stirred the desire to undertake the task of writing this study of the book of the prophet Ezekiel.

Clifford Hill
February 2024

1 THE CONDEMNATION OF JERUSALEM
Ezekiel 22:1-7

This is what the Sovereign Lord says: "O city that brings on itself doom by shedding blood in her midst and defiles herself by making idols, you have become guilty because of the blood you have shed and have become defiled by the idols you have made . . ."

The oracle in this passage is a condemnation of the city of Jerusalem which is preparing the way for news of its destruction that comes as an enormous shock to the exiles in Babylon. Ezekiel has to justify God's action in allowing the tragedy. The first charge is that of blood-guilt, which is a sin that the prophets of Israel had regularly condemned since the 8th century. Micah said that Zion was built on bloodshed and Jerusalem was filled with wickedness (Mic 3:10) and Hosea said that the whole land was filled with bloodshed. *"There is only cursing, lying and murder, stealing and adultery; they break all bounds and bloodshed follows bloodshed"* (Hos 4:2).

In the history of Israel, it is stated that the reason why God allowed Jerusalem to be invaded by the Babylonians was because of *"the sins of Manasseh and all he had done including the shedding of innocent blood. For he filled Jerusalem with innocent blood and the Lord was not willing to forgive"* (2 Kgs 24:3-4). Manasseh began his reign in 696, exactly 100 years before Zedekiah. Clearly, the history of Jerusalem as a city of bloodshed went back a long way and showed the patience of God.

The indictment of Jerusalem was a divine judgement upon the whole society for its bloodshed, idolatry, and immorality. This was very similar to the list of sins of Jerusalem given by Jeremiah in his famous 'temple sermon'. Jeremiah included injustice and oppression and false religion (Jer 7:1-11). Ezekiel refers to the sins of the princes of Israel, which is a generic term to include all those who held power in the city from the monarchy to the priests and prophets. They were all guilty of breaking the commandments of God.

The men of Jerusalem were accused of acts of idolatry by going up into the mountain shrines where there were sex temples practising fertility rites. They indulged in sexual acts that were specifically forbidden in the Law given through Moses. They added to their sins by injustice, accepting bribes, and extortion and usury.

All their social relationships were unjust and crooked, and in their family life there was adultery and personal corruption. Jeremiah had stated this, he said, as a word from God, *"Among the prophets of Jerusalem I have seen something horrible: they commit adultery and live a lie. They strengthen the hands of evildoers, so that no one turns from his wickedness. They are like Sodom to me, the people of Jerusalem are like Gomorrah"* (Jer 23:14).

Over and above all their wickedness, the people had forgotten their God. This picture of society that the whole city was guilty before God of such utter corruption was so shocking that it led to God striking his hands together as a gesture of condemnation of the city that he had graced with his presence and had divinely protected in the past. This signalled God's intention of dispersing the population of Jerusalem and the surrounding area of Judah among the nations.

By driving the people into exile, God would be putting an end to their uncleanness and the destruction of Jerusalem would be seen by all the nations, both those who were near neighbours, and by others far away. The desecration of the city would be an international disgrace that all the citizens of Jerusalem would have to bear. They would be forced to recognise that they had brought this tragedy upon themselves by defying all the warnings they had been given. When all this happened, the people of Israel would be forced to recognise the hand of the Lord that had fallen upon them justly, and more importantly, the name of God would be justified in the eyes of the Gentiles.

This is an important passage of Scripture for giving us an understanding of the nature and purposes of God. It has special significance in terms of the justice of God. It shows that even with the people of Israel whom he chose out of all the nations of the world to be his servants, he would exercise judgement upon them under extreme circumstances.

Israel was chosen to be his servant through whom he would reveal himself to the nations. To enable them to fulfil their servanthood, he made a covenant with them that required total obedience. In return, he would protect them and pour out his blessings and give prosperity. The history of Israel shows the truth of this – when the nation was righteous they prospered, but when they were unrighteous they suffered.

2 THE SOCIAL DISORDER OF JERUSALEM
Ezekiel 22: 8-16

"You have despised my holy things and desecrated my Sabbaths. In you are slanderous men bent on shedding blood; in you are those who eat at the mountain shrines and commit lewd acts . . . In you men accept bribes to shed blood, you take usury . . ."

The word given to Ezekiel in verse 6 of this chapter is about the 'princes'. We have already noted that this was a generic term referring to all those who held some kind of power or influence in the nation's capital. They were not only the monarch and his 'council of reference', but all those who held some sort of influence in society such as politicians, community elders, or commercial leaders. They were the ones who were primarily responsible for 'forgetting God' and committing a wide range of sins and not setting a good example to the people so that even the basic terms of the covenant were neglected.

The central charge against the leadership in Jerusalem was that they despised the holy things of God and desecrated his Sabbaths. They were living in total disregard for all the moral and spiritual requirements of the Lord, despising the observance of God's Sabbaths. The list of offences in the city was shocking. There were *"slanderous men bent on shedding blood"*. Slander was banned as offensive in terms of human relationships according to Leviticus 19:16. The shedding of blood was offensive to God in every generation as in the days of Manasseh who filled the city with innocent blood (2 Kgs 21:16).

Men went up into the mountain shrines to use the services of shrine prostitutes and other detestable activities that were available there. The men committed all kinds of sexual sins and they had turned the city of Jerusalem into some kind of brothel - which was utterly obnoxious to God. The list of banned sexual offences was set out in Leviticus 18. At the end of the list of banned sexual relationships there was a strong warning. *"Do not defile yourselves in any of these ways, because this is how the nations that I am going to drive out before you became defiled"* (Lev 18:24).

This was a salutary warning of the judgement that would fall upon the land if these warnings about sexual relationships were ignored. The men in the city of Jerusalem continued to commit detestable offences with their neighbours' wives, and shamefully defiled their daughters-in-law and other members of their family. The moral state of the nation was incredibly low from the description that Ezekiel gives.

Men with leading responsibilities in the city were involved in bloodshed to a shocking degree. They even hired other men to go and commit murder on their behalf, and they had no code of morality in their business practices where they took usury and excessive interest making unjust gain from their neighbours by extortion. All these things showed a complete disregard for the value of relationships in the community which was highly displeasing to God. He would express his anger by striking his hands together, condemning all the unjust actions that were taking place in the city that was clearly in a state of social decay, provoking God to exercise judgement.

The word of the Lord to all these men who were disregarding the teaching that had been given to them since the time of Moses was, *"Will your courage endure or your hands be strong in the day I deal with you? I the Lord have spoken, and I will do it."* The threat was that God would disperse the people among the nations and put an end to their uncleanness. The whole population of the city of Jerusalem would be shamed in the eyes of the world, and this would be a demonstration of the justice of God.

The destruction that came upon the city was certainly in accordance with the threats in this passage. The statement that the people of Jerusalem would be defiled in the eyes of the nations is referred to in many statements after the fall of Jerusalem, *"Jerusalem has become an unclean thing among them"* (Lam 1:17). *"They are so defiled with blood that no one dares to touch their garments. Go away! You are unclean! Men cry to them. Away! Away! Do not touch us!"* (Lam 4:14-15).

The terrible fulfilment of the pronouncement of judgement in the words of Ezekiel in chapter 22 was recognised after the destruction of the city in 586. *"It happened because of the sins of her prophets and the iniquities of her priests who shed within her the blood of the righteous"* (Lam 4:13). The Lord's promise to strike his hands together and to exercise judgement upon the sins of Jerusalem was certainly fulfilled.

3 THE SMELTING FURNACE AND DROSS
Ezekiel 22:17-22

Then the word of the Lord came to me: "Son of man, the house of Israel has become dross to me; all of them are the copper, tin, iron and lead left inside a furnace. They are but the dross of silver . . ."

In the first half of this chapter Ezekiel was reporting on what he was hearing from God about the whole population of Jerusalem and Judah who had become offensive to God through their wickedness. They had forgotten the God of Israel, the God of their fathers who had done so many wonderful things in the life of the nation. Now Jerusalem was about to suffer because God was saying that he was at the end of his patience with them. He would withdraw his protection and the people would be scattered among the nations and, for those to whom Ezekiel was ministering in Babylon, this had already happened.

Something dreadful was going to happen to Jerusalem and all those who remained within her walls. She would be like a furnace used for smelting silver to get rid of all the impurities. Some of the exiles would have seen silver being purified and they would remember the enormous heat needed to liquefy the silver and the bits of copper, iron, and lead, left as dross in the furnace.

It was a terrible metaphor for the city, that God in his fiery wrath would blow fire upon them. They would have remembered their elders recounting the days of slavery in Egypt which were regarded as being in a fiery furnace from which the Lord God had wonderfully rescued them (Jer 11:4).

Now God was promising to reverse all that. He was withdrawing his protection, leaving them to face the fiery furnace that the Babylonians would pour out upon them. This was the 'wrath of God' which occurs more in the Book of Ezekiel than in any other book in the Bible. This is because the central theme of Ezekiel's work is to teach about the holiness of God and that the sinfulness of human beings puts us outside the light and truth and beauty and blessings of God – that is his wrath – being separated from God.

Instead of teaching the Torah to the people and setting an example of righteousness and faithful servanthood, the leaders had used their power for exploitation, devouring people's livelihoods, taking their precious possessions, shedding innocent blood, and creating widows and orphans. The leadership of the people of Jerusalem had laid bare the spiritual barrenness of the nation and this was why they were already a nation under judgement.

The judgement had begun by God withholding the rain in due season which had inevitably affected harvests and created food shortages and suffering. Shortages also create competition for things in short supply. Instead of regulations designed to create fairness in society, the leaders had misused their power to feed themselves while others were hungry, bringing judgement upon them.

The drought was not only hitting Judah, but all the region we now know as the 'Middle-East' – from Lebanon to the eastern borders of Iran. Climatologists tell us that there was a period of global warming in that area in the 6th century BC that was turning much of Babylonia into desert which is one of the factors that would influence Nebuchadnezzar to seek forced labour to dig canals for a massive irrigation system to revolutionise his agriculture and feed the hungry population.

The weapons of judgement to which the prophets often referred were drought, famine, disease, and war. All these were part of the judgement that was now falling upon Judah as God turned his face away from his people. This was the picture that Ezekiel was seeing and describing to the elders who would have been fearing for their families back in Judah. It was part of the lessons that they were having to learn before they could become a cleansed and redeemed people.

The terrible truth that Ezekiel was having to convey to the elders in Babylon was that judgement was going to fall upon their families, friends, and neighbours back in Jerusalem. It would be – "*As men gather silver, copper, iron, lead and tin into a furnace to melt it with a fiery blast, so will I gather you in my anger and my wrath and put you inside the city and melt you*" *(v. 20)*. This was the wrath of God that was going to descend upon the city that was the inevitable result of their sinfulness in driving God out of the city which left it open to the forces of darkness. God himself would be grieving deeply for the suffering of his beloved people – this was his wrath, anger, grief, and love all poured out upon the city he loved.

4 UNFAITHFUL PROPHETS Ezekiel 22:23-26

Again the word of the Lord came to me: 'Son of man, say to the land, you are a land that has had no rain or showers in the day of wrath. There is a conspiracy of her princes within her like a roaring lion tearing its prey . . ."

Among all the hard words of condemnation in this chapter this is the hardest word of all. As we have already observed, the drought had signalled the beginning of the day of wrath. Now the full wrath of God was about to begin. The conspiracy among the ruling elite through a refusal to face the truth was misusing the civic power that had been entrusted to them. They were devouring the people; truth and justice had disappeared from the streets of Jerusalem as in Isaiah's day, *"righteousness stands at a distance; truth has stumbled in the streets"* (Is 59:14).

Everywhere there was exploitation as leaders used their positions for personal gain and shedding blood to get what they wanted. There was no justice in the courts as bribery and corruption ruled the day. If the poor did go to court the judge had already been bribed by the rich, so there was no justice for the poor. The conspiracy referred to here is not Zedekiah's revolt against Babylon. The leaders of the nation were involved in a far more serious conspiracy – it was a conspiracy against the Lord!

Ezekiel then turns to the most serious accusation – the priests in the temple who were part of the aristocracy of Jerusalem were in revolt against God. They were distorting the Torah and profaning God's holy things. This was the charge that Jeremiah had levelled at the priests and prophets in Jerusalem. He said that the scribes mishandled the word of God to suit their own purposes and as a consequence of their unfaithfulness the people did not know the requirements of the Lord. He said, *"How can you say, we are wise for we have the law of the Lord, when actually the lying pen of the scribes has handled it falsely?"* He said, *"Since they have rejected the word of the Lord, what kind of wisdom do they have?"* (Jer 8:8-9). Jeremiah said, *"prophets and priests alike, all practice deceit."* (Jer 6:13)

Ezekiel now echoed this, *"Her priests do violence to my law and profane my holy things, they do not distinguish between the holy and the common, they teach the people that there is no difference between the clean and the unclean"* (v. 26). He knew that the scribes were mistranslating the Torah to suit their own purposes – he had seen it as a student, and he knew the corruption that existed in the temple. Looking back, he must have wondered why he had not said something about it at the time. How he must have wished that he could have talked with Jeremiah! If he had joined with Jeremiah, could they have made a difference in the nation?

The final charge against the priests and prophets (or preachers) was that they did not give right teaching to the people particularly in respect of the requirements of the Torah. Isaiah had made a similar accusation about the teachers of the Law. His pronouncement was, *"Woe to those who call evil good and good evil, who put darkness for light and light for darkness"* (Is 5:20). That was in 8th century Jerusalem – some 200 years earlier, but things had not changed.

Ezekiel's charge against the priests and prophets of Jerusalem was that they were Sabbath-breakers. This was the most serious charge of all. In the eyes of God, his Sabbaths were the sign of his covenant with the people of Israel. The keeping of the Sabbath as a day that was different from all the rest of the working week was essential as an acknowledgement by the nation that the God of Israel was of supreme importance in the lives of the people of Israel.

The Lord had said to Moses, *"Say to the Israelites, you must observe my Sabbaths. This will be a sign between me and you for the generations to come, so you may know that I am the Lord, who makes you holy"* [different from the world] (Ex 31:12-13). Ezekiel taught that the Sabbath was given by God as a sign of the covenant between God and his people. He reminded the exiles of God's words to the Israelites in the wilderness, *"Do not follow the statutes of your parents or keep their laws or defile yourselves with their idols. I am the Lord your God; follow my decrees and be careful to keep my laws. Keep my Sabbaths holy, that they may be a sign between us"* (Ezek 20:18-19).

5 STANDING IN THE GAP Ezekiel 22:27-31

Her officials within her are like wolves tearing their prey; they shed blood and kill people to make unjust gain. Her prophets whitewash these deeds for them by false visions and lying divinations.

In this final section of chapter 22 Ezekiel turns the focus upon the religious leaders of Jerusalem. This is familiar territory for him because he was one of them. We know nothing of his early life, but we know that he was a priest and part of the temple community in Jerusalem who were part of the aristocracy and closely linked with the monarchy. Ezekiel must have seen many things going on in the temple that he had become accustomed to, and that he now realised actually profaned the holy things of God. He would have been one of the priests who were bitterly criticised by Jeremiah. *"From the least to the greatest, all are greedy for gain; prophets and priests alike all practice deceit"* (Jer 6:13).

Jeremiah also said, *"Both prophet and priest are godless; even in my temple I find their wickedness, declares the Lord . . . Among the prophets of Jerusalem, I have seen something horrible; they commit adultery and live a lie. They strengthen the hands of evildoers so that no one turns from his wickedness . . . From the prophets of Jerusalem ungodliness has spread throughout the land"* (Jer 23:11-15). What Jeremiah regarded as even worse than their adulterous behaviour was the fact that they gave wrong spiritual teaching to the leaders and to the people of Jerusalem, thereby endangering the whole city. He said, *"They fill you with false hopes. They speak visions from their own minds not from the mouth of the Lord . . . They say, 'No harm will come to you.' But which of them has stood in the council of the Lord to see or hear his word?"* (Jer 23:16-18).

Even though Ezekiel, like the majority of the priests, rejected the teaching of Jeremiah, there is plenty of evidence that he had scrolls of Jeremiah's teaching with him in Babylon and slowly he was changing his teaching to bring it more in line with Jeremiah's. He clearly also had a scroll of Zephaniah whose teaching he may have remembered from the time of King Josiah when he was active in Jerusalem. He may have taken this scroll with him when he left the temple and was taken to Babylon. Zephaniah chapter 3 is clearly linked to the reading we are studying today in Ezekiel 22. The reference to *"Her rulers are evening wolves who leave nothing for the morning . . . Her priests profane the sanctuary and do violence to the law"* (Zeph 3:3-4). This is linked to Ezekiel's charge *"Her priests do violence to my law and profane my holy things; they do not distinguish between the holy and the common."* (v. 26)

This was something particularly important to Ezekiel in emphasising the need for holiness in his teaching of the elders of Israel in exile. Central to his teaching is this concept of holiness – of Israel being separated from the nations, different from the world. He realised that the priests among whom he had been taught in Jerusalem were not practising this basic teaching that was at the heart of the covenant relationship between God and the people of Israel.

Ezekiel knew that both priests and prophets in Jerusalem failed to keep the Sabbaths and thus profaned the God of Israel. *"They shed blood and kill people to make unjust gain"* which may be a reference to the priests charging money for teaching people the word of the Lord. Like Jeremiah, he had actually seen the leaders of the land practising extortion and committing robbery by oppressing the poor and needy and ill-treating the alien, denying them justice.

The treatment of aliens was an important sign of the standards of justice in the nation. It was a basic requirement of God. *"Do not ill-treat an alien or oppress him, for you were aliens in Egypt"* (Ex 22:21). The leadership in Jerusalem, including the priests, cared for no one except themselves. Their standards of justice were an offence to God.

The most terrible thing in the memory of Ezekiel from his days of priesthood at the temple in Jerusalem, was that God was looking for righteous men who would be intercessors on behalf of the nation. He wanted men who would stand in the gap on behalf of the land which could have stayed the hand of the Lord in judgement upon the city. Apart from Jeremiah, who had been rejected by all his fellow priests and by the ruling party in the monarchy, Ezekiel could think of no one who was righteous in the eyes of the Lord. There was no one to pray for the peace of Jerusalem. This was Jerusalem's tragedy and the tragedy of the people of Judah.

6 TWO ADULTEROUS SISTERS Ezekiel 23:1-31

The word of the Lord came to me: "Son of man, there were two women, daughters of the same mother. They became prostitutes in Egypt, engaging in prostitution from their youth . . . The older was named Oholah, and her sister was Oholibah. They were mine and gave birth to sons and daughters. Oholah is Samaria, and Oholibah is Jerusalem. Oholah engaged in prostitution while she was still mine, and she lusted after her lovers, the Assyrians. Therefore I handed her over to her lovers, the Assyrians. Her sister Oholibah saw this, yet in her lust and prostitution she was more depraved than her sister."

The whole of chapter 23 is a single section in the form of an allegory of two adulterous sisters. They are the two kingdoms of Israel in the north and Judah in the south. The chapter traces the history of the two kingdoms from the time the nation of Israel became divided during the reign of Rehoboam, to the end of each of them. The prophets generally regard the whole of this period of the division between North and South as being a time when the people of Israel were under judgement. God removed his cover of protection over both of them, which led first to judgement and exile falling upon Samaria and then upon Jerusalem. We will take the chapter in two halves, dealing with an overview of the chapter and then more specifically on the message in each half.

There is a strong connection between this chapter and chapter 16 which also is a condemnation of Jerusalem's sinfulness. The difference between the two is that chapter 16 refers to the idolatry and religious waywardness of Jerusalem, whereas this chapter is a condemnation of the whole nation of Israel, both north and south, and their political alliances which are seen as treachery against Yahweh the God of Israel. In Ezekiel's view any alliance with other nations shows a lack of trust in God and is therefore a spiritual offence amounting to idolatry – putting their trust in human alliances instead of total trust in the God of Israel who had made covenant promises at Mount Sinai.

The first half of the chapter, verses 1-32 develops an allegory with various literary devices to analyse the sins of the two nations of Israel and Judah. The figures of the lovers in the allegory become the instrument of destruction for each of them. There are four parts in the allegory: verses 2-4 cover the childhood of the two sisters in Egypt. Verses 5-10 is the story of the elder sister Israel. Verses 11-21 are the story of the younger sister Judah, and verses 22-31 are the judgements that come upon each of them. The second half of the chapter, verses 32–49 is a further interpretation of the allegory dealing with the history of the two nations and the punishment that they brought upon themselves through their spiritual adultery and running after the gods of the other nations.

Verse 3 says that their prostitution began in Egypt. It is not clear what this means: it may be a reference to the time of slavery in Egypt when many of the people worshipped Egyptian idols. It may refer to the fact that King Solomon married an Egyptian princess and gave her provisions for worshipping her Egyptian gods. *"On a hill east of Jerusalem, Solomon built a high place for Chemosh the detestable God of Moab, and for Molech the detestable God of the Amorites. He did the same for all his foreign wives, who burned incense and offered sacrifices to their gods"* (1 Kgs 11:7-8).

Verse 5 *"while she was mine"* refers to the northern kingdom of Israel during the period before 722 and the fall of Samaria, after which the Assyrians brought in people from other parts of their empire and produced a mixed population. They became the Samaritans – so they were no longer exclusively the family of Israel with whom God had made a covenant at Mount Sinai.

This is confirmed in verse 10 where the Assyrians *"took away her sons and daughters"* and brought in other communities from around the Assyrian Empire. In verse 11 Oholibah, Jerusalem, becomes even more depraved than her sister Samaria, entering into alliances with both the Babylonians and the Egyptians. The *'men on the wall'* in verse 14 are the Babylonians. Verse 27 says that God's intention is to put a stop to all the idolatry that began in Egypt. He was going to hand over both sisters to those they had lusted after and with whom they had defiled themselves. They would now be their downfall. They had brought all this upon themselves because they lusted after the nations and defiled themselves with their idols.

7 MORE ABOUT THE TWO SISTERS
Ezekiel 23:32-49

This is what the Sovereign Lord says: "You will drink your sister's cup, a cup large and deep; it will bring scorn and derision, for it holds so much."

Both of the sisters will suffer at the hands of their lovers which is the theme of the little poem that is developed in verses 32–34. It is addressed to the southern kingdom of Judah and it says that they will be filled with drunkenness and sorrow because *"the cup of ruin and desolation, the cup of your sister Samaria"* will be given to them to drink and they will drain it dry. The judgement that had already come upon Israel whose population had been scattered across the Assyrian empire would now fall upon Judah. The reason for this is summarised in verse 35, "*Since you have forgotten me and thrust me behind your back, you must bear the consequences of your lewdness and prostitution.*"

Ezekiel was instructed to confront Jerusalem with the detestable practices that they had committed which included idolatry and the shedding of innocent blood – the most detestable crime of sacrificing their babies and desecrating the land. Jeremiah had raged against the terrible idolatry of the people who hoped to appease the Babylonians by worshipping some of their gods. There were rumours that their army was on the way to attack Jerusalem and the people had no faith in God to save them. Jeremiah was told, *"This is the nation that has not obeyed the Lord its God or responded to correction. Truth has perished, it has vanished from their lips."* Therefore, he was told, *"The Lord has rejected and abandoned this generation that is under his wrath"* (Jer 7:28-29).

Ezekiel is thought to be referring to the same episode as Jeremiah when he says, *"At that same time they defiled my sanctuary and desecrated my Sabbaths. On the very day they sacrificed their children to their idols, they entered my sanctuary and defiled it. That is what they did in my house"* (Ezek 23:38-39). Jeremiah had said that at the same time as they went out to the Valley of Ben Hinnom to burn their babies they had *"set up their detestable idols in the house that bears my name and defiled it"* (Jer 7:30). All these things were so heinous in the eyes of God that he could do no other than turn his back upon them.

Ezekiel foresaw the terrible judgement that was going to come upon the city that he loved and where he had spent his childhood and youth. He must have remembered the desecration of the temple and the burning of babies. It is almost certain that he would have had a copy of Jeremiah's scroll with him in Babylon and Jeremiah's condemnation of the events that he himself would have remembered, would have been burned into his memory. It was perfectly clear to him that God was fully justified in allowing terrible judgement to come upon his people. He describes the fearful atrocities that he has heard that the Babylonian soldiers committed as they raped and pillaged when they had finally broken through the walls into the city of Jerusalem. This is what he is describing in verses 43 and 44 which he sees as a judgement upon the adulterous who have the blood of the innocent on their hands.

Verses 36–49 are extremely difficult to translate because of corruption in the Hebrew text. Verses such as 42 and 43 are virtually untranslatable. The AV and NIV say *"Sabeans were brought in from the desert"*, but the NRSV says, *"many of the rabble [were] brought in drunken from the wilderness."* The Hebrew may mean either 'Sabeans' or 'drunkards'. The AV speaks of a company stoning the sisters as a recompense for their lewdness, and them bearing the sins of their idolatry, whereas the NIV speaks of a mob stoning, killing, and burning them as a penalty for their sins.

Ezekiel foresees the Babylonians bringing death and destruction to Jerusalem. They would cut the people down with their swords, *"they will kill their sons and daughters and burn down their houses".* All this terrible judgement will be allowed by God, *"so I will put an end to lewdness in the land, that all women may take warning and not imitate you."* The chapter ends with the terrible indictment, *"You will suffer the penalty for your lewdness and bear the consequences of your sins of idolatry. Then you will know that I am the Sovereign Lord."* In reading this as a word from God it must be remembered that the prophets do not distinguish between the direct will of God and the allowable will of God. In this case God has allowed it as the inevitable outcome of the sinfulness of his people, but his grief is indescribable.

8 THE COOKING POT Ezekiel 24: 1-14

In the ninth year, in the tenth month on the tenth day, the word of the Lord came to me. "Son of man, record this date, this very date, because the King of Babylon has laid siege to Jerusalem this very day. Tell this rebellious house a parable . . ."

Ezekiel chapter 24 is in two parts – verses 1-14 and 15-27. Today we are covering the first section which is yet another allegory. It begins with a date, January 588, the day that Nebuchadnezzar began his siege of the city of Jerusalem, which was observed as a day of fasting from the time of the exile, as we learn from Zechariah 8:19. Ezekiel recalls it as a day of judgement upon the rebellious house of Israel, but how did Ezekiel, far away in Babylon, know the exact time when Nebuchadnezzar began his siege of Jerusalem?

Of course, the date could have been added later, which is what most biblical scholars conclude, but Ezekiel records this as a prophetic word that he received from God. There is no reason to doubt him because all the people of Judah in exile would have known when the Babylonian army left Babylon. Ezekiel would have known how long it would take them to reach Jerusalem and he would no doubt have been counting off the days and been highly alert to receive any word from the Lord.

The allegory of verses 3-5 is of a cooking pot with choice pieces of meat and the bones all put into the pot which is placed on a pile of burning wood. This is a little allegorical poem which may have been well known among the exiles. Ezekiel gives the interpretation of it in verses 9 and 10 – *"Woe to the city of bloodshed! I, too, will pile the wood high. So heap on the wood and kindle the fire. Cook the meat well."*

The interpretation is obviously a reference to Jerusalem, now under siege. Ezekiel had already recorded the glory of the Lord leaving the temple, and Jerusalem was now unprotected and left open to the enemy for destruction. Verse 14 underlines this *"I the Lord have spoken. The time has come for me to act. I will not hold back; I will not have pity, nor will I relent."* Judgement day for Jerusalem has come.

The sins of Manasseh, who had filled the city with the blood of the innocent, was now bringing retribution upon the rebellious city that had turned its back upon God and was relying upon Egypt to come to their aid. Jeremiah tells us how Nebuchadnezzar withdrew his army from around Jerusalem when he heard that the Egyptian army was on the move. But Jeremiah said, "*I am going to give the order, declares the Lord, and I will bring them back to this city. They will fight against it, take it, and burn it down. And I will lay waste the towns of Judah so that no one can live there*" (Jer 34:21-22).

Ezekiel then brings in another little poem about the city of bloodshed, in verses 6-8. It is about an old pot that becomes encrusted. The city of Jerusalem is a city of strife and rebellion against God. God has sent prophets, one after another for many years in an attempt to cleanse the city from its impurity, but the word of the Lord given through them has been ignored. The impurities have grown like those in an old pot. They have become visible to everyone, like blood being spilled onto bare rock, so that it could not be covered. The city of iniquity could be seen by all the world, so in the end God pronounced his judgement upon the rebellious city.

The empty pot is set on the fire, "*until it becomes hot and its copper glows so that its impurities may be melted and its deposit burned away.*" The whole allegory is given in the first person singular as a word from God. The RSV translates verse 12 as 'rust' but the Hebrew does not say this because copper does not rust. The AV calls it 'scum', but the NIV is more accurate with 'heavy deposit'. Then God said, "*Your impurity is lewdness. Because I tried to cleanse you but you would not be cleansed from your impurity, you will not be clean again until my wrath against you has subsided.*"

God's purposes in taking so many from Judah into exile and raising up Ezekiel amongst them, was to create a faithful remnant of believers who would come back to the promised land when Babylon came to an end – cleansed and purified and now with a new heart and a new spirit – the Spirit of the Lord – to prepare the way for the new Jerusalem.

9 EZEKIEL'S WIFE DIES Ezekiel 24:15-26

The word of the Lord came to me: "Son of man, with one blow I am about to take away from you the delight of your eyes. Yet do not lament or weep or shed any tears. Groan quietly, do not mourn for the dead. Keep your turban fastened and your sandals on your feet; do not cover the lower part of your face or eat the customary food of mourners." So I spoke to the people in the morning, and in the evening my wife died. The next morning I did as I had been commanded.

At the beginning of this passage Jeremiah is warned that suddenly and in the near future, his wife is to die, but he is not to mourn for her. At the same time, he is warned that the temple in Jerusalem will shortly be destroyed. The phrase *"the delight of your eyes"* is used in both forewarnings. This day will bring about these two momentous events as one blow. Ezekiel was told that he should not weep in public but do his crying quietly with no public mourning.

He spoke to the people as usual in the morning. The script does not say that this was a Sabbath, but it was certainly an occasion when the preacher was expected to speak to the people and not just to the elders as he did when they came to his home. That same evening his wife died. Presumably this was a sudden death, perhaps from a stroke because there is no hint of previous illness.

The following morning Ezekiel went about as usual although, the death of his wife must, by this time already have become known, because people were asking him why he was not undertaking the customary mourning by removing his head covering and his sandals and covering the lower part of his face. This gave Ezekiel the opportunity for speaking publicly and declaring openly that he had heard from God that the temple in Jerusalem that was their pride and joy, *'the delight of their eyes'*, was going to be destroyed. What was more, their families and friends back home in Jerusalem were going to be slaughtered by the swords of the Babylonian army.

Ezekiel went on to say that it was the word of the Lord to them that they also should follow him in not undertaking any public mourning. *"You will not mourn or weep but will waste away because of your sins and groan among yourselves."* (v. 23). This will be their act of repentance before God, acknowledging the justice of God in removing his cover of protection from over the temple and allowing it to be destroyed. This was an act of God in taking away *"their stronghold, their joy and glory, the delight of their eyes".* They must not mourn in public allowing the Babylonians to see their sorrow so they could say that their gods had triumphed over the God of Israel. He was, in fact, in full control – and he was working out his purposes, allowing Jerusalem to be cleansed.

The reference to *'their stronghold'* is significant because many of the exiles still regarded the temple as the place where the presence of God remained and therefore, he would defend it. Ezekiel had been trying to teach the elders that God was present among them in Babylon – and now they were going to have to stop relying upon the morning and evening sacrifice in the temple to deal with the sins of the nation. They had to accept Ezekiel's teaching of individual responsibility. This was still early days in the exile before the development of the Synagogue, when family worship and prayers over the Shabbat meal were just developing, and the gatherings in the meeting places (knessets) had not yet been established in all the settlements.

The final verses in this section are addressed to Ezekiel himself telling him that when the siege is broken and the city of Jerusalem is destroyed he will receive news from a fugitive escaping the destruction. This will be a justification for all the abuse and opposition he has encountered for his warnings to the exiles.

It is possible that Ezekiel was struck dumb from this point, or instructed not to speak in public, or to the elders again, until the word of the Lord he had been proclaiming about the destruction of Jerusalem is fulfilled. Then he would be released from all restrictions and be able to declare the word of God with power and authority. In Ezekiel 3:24-27 the prophet had been given forewarning of this. He had been told that he would be silent for a period, but when God opened his mouth the word of the Lord would be recognised by all those who heard him. That day had not yet come – but it was near!

10 THE ORACLES AGAINST THE NATIONS
Ezekiel 25:1 – 32:16

No longer will the people of Israel have malicious neighbours who are painful briars and sharp thorns. Then they will know that I am the Sovereign Lord. (Ezek 28:24)

This is an additional note on the eight chapters, Ezekiel 25 – 32. They are quite different from the main chapters of Ezekiel's teaching including his visions, anagrams, and interpretations. The oracles in these chapters are carefully crafted to bring a message of comfort and hope to the exiles in Babylon. The use of groups of seven is significant and it would have conveyed a message of well-being and assurance from God to the exiles, which was much needed in the immediate aftermath of the shock news of the destruction of Jerusalem.

The use of seven is a regular feature of the Hebrew prophets in their teaching such as Amos who divided his teaching to the people of Israel into seven parts in his opening address to the crowds. He directed his words against six neighbouring nations before coming to the seventh – which was Judah. The crowds would have loved it when Amos brought the word of the Lord against Damascus, Gaza, Tyre, Edom, Moab, and most of all against their sister nation Judah! Then he turned his fire upon Israel which was the whole purpose of his prophetic mission.

In the same mode of teaching, Ezekiel named the neighbours who deserted Israel in their hour of need. They had all been erstwhile allies of Israel, but each had failed to support when needed, leaving Judah alone to face the wrath of Babylon. The seven nations were Ammon (25:1-7), Moab (25:8-11, Edom (25:12-14), Philistia (25:15-17), Tyre (26:1-28:19), Sidon (28:20-23), Egypt (29:1-32). The naming of all seven nations is not a buildup to any critical statement on Israel, but the seven is a symbol of comfort of God's word against those who had become enemies of Israel.

Among the exiles there was great anger against each of these seven neighbouring nations whose offences are elaborated here. This whole section has been carefully constructed with the central point in the eight chapters being 28:24-26. These three verses provide the key to understanding the whole section. This is why we are dealing with it here because it has central significance. Its opening phrase is a direct word of comfort to the exiles. It says *"No longer will the people of Israel have malicious neighbours who are painful briars and sharp thorns. Then they will know that I am the Sovereign Lord."*

This is followed by a direct reference to the end of the exile when God would take his people back to the land, which is the first reference Ezekiel has made to this promise. It sets out the theme that Ezekiel will elaborate later showing God's purpose in sending his people into exile. *"I will show myself holy among them in the sight of the nations."* There follows further direct promises of blessings and prosperity which God will give to them when they are back in the land and living there in safety.

This is followed by a promise that God would bring retribution on the neighbouring nations who had not only failed to support Israel in their time of need, but they had actually maligned Yahweh the God of Israel. God's action in restoring his people to the promised land and blessing them with prosperity would reveal the power of God and his nature of justice and loving forgiveness. He would be seen as totally different from all the gods of the nations. Through this the 'holiness' of God would be the outstanding feature of God's nature revealed to the Gentiles. Once again the words are repeated, *"Then they will know that I am the Lord their God."*

This is the whole purpose of this section around 28:24-26 showing that God had not deserted them. He was still Sovereign Lord of the nations, and he was comforting his people in exile who were in Babylon for a purpose. The verses either side of this central message each add up to 97.[2] This is part of the carefully constructed message that Ezekiel is giving to reassure the exiles of the sovereignty of God who is watching over them for their good despite the destruction of Jerusalem that he has allowed.

2 I am grateful to Christopher Wright for pointing this out, although he does not elaborate on the significance. (Christopher Wright, 'The Message of Ezekiel', Inter-Varsity Press, Nottingham, 2001, page 230.) I am not an expert in Hebrew numerology, so I cannot offer any explanation for this, but I can recognise that the use of 'sevens' throughout this part of the Book of Ezekiel would have conveyed a message of comfort to the exiles.

11 A MESSAGE AGAINST AMMON Ezekiel 25:1-7

The word of the Lord came to me: "Son of man, set your face against the Ammonites and prophesy against them. Say to them, hear the word of the Sovereign Lord. This is what the Sovereign Lord says: Because you said, 'Aha!' over my sanctuary when it was desecrated . . ."

All the messages in this sector of eight chapters have a similar theme and cover the period of history immediately following the destruction of Jerusalem in 586. It is a period for which historical records are very sparse. The best source of information which covers a period of about 10 years after the destruction of Jerusalem, is to be found in Jeremiah chapters 40 to 44. These show Jeremiah's struggle to persuade the survivors of the disaster to stay in the land following the slaughter carried out by the Babylonian army after they broke through the walls of Jerusalem at the end of the two-year siege. The Babylonians appointed Gedaliah as Governor of the province of Judah before they withdrew to Babylon, leaving a small garrison of soldiers with him to secure the region.

Gedaliah set up his residence at Mizpah, some 4 miles north-west of Jerusalem, up in the hill country where there were plenty of vineyards producing summer fruit, wine, and oil that had been spared by the Babylonians. Ishmael, who was said to be of royal blood, took a small group of 10 men to visit Gedaliah where they treacherously killed him while being entertained to a meal. According to Jeremiah's report, *"Ishmael also killed all the Jews who were with Gedaliah at Mizpah, as well as the Babylonian soldiers who were there"* (Jer 41:3).

It was a highly unstable period with no government or army to ensure national stability which left the country open for exploitation from neighbouring nations, such as Ammon, Moab and Edom who were all clearly delighted at the fall of Judah and the destruction of Jerusalem. They openly laughed at the plight of the people and indulged in looting the city, which is a major reason why there was such animosity towards them reflected in the prophecies presented in these chapters of Ezekiel. It is essential to understand this period of history in order to appreciate the oracles against the nations that Ezekiel is declaring.

In this chapter two short pieces of doom against Ammon are put together, and these are followed by short words against Moab, Edom, and Philistia. Both the Moabites and the Ammonites had sent detachments of soldiers to join the Babylonian army in the attack upon Jerusalem in 598 according to 2 Kings 24:1-2. This is what infuriated the people of Judah which is reflected in this passage by Ezekiel. King Jehoiakim had been paying taxes to Babylon for three years and then foolishly he revolted against Babylon shortly before he died. Nebuchadnezzar then sent a combined army of Babylonian and other soldiers against Jerusalem. The report in 2 Kings 24:3 says, *"Surely these things happened to Judah according to the Lord's command, in order to remove them from his presence because of the sins of Manasseh."*

This was a highly unstable period in the history of Judah and the surrounding nations. They had to change their loyalty between the three warring empires of Assyria, Babylon, and Egypt. But just five years after the attack upon Jerusalem, in 593 both Moab and Ammon joined Egypt to take part in a conspiracy to revolt against Babylon which is described in Jeremiah 27. This infuriated Nebuchadnezzar and he set out to attack both Judah and Ammon. He stopped at the junction of two roads according to the report in Ezekiel 21:21 to decide which to attack first. He chose Jerusalem and in 588 he began the two-year siege of the city and the devastation of the towns and villages across the land of Judah.

Although Ammon did not take part in the attack upon Jerusalem this time, as soon as the walls of Jerusalem were broken, people flocked across the River Jordan to take part in looting the towns of Judah and the city of Jerusalem. They actually rejoiced to see the destruction of the temple which particularly angered Yahweh who said, *"Because you have clapped your hands and stamped your feet, rejoicing with all the malice of your heart against the land of Israel, therefore I will stretch out my hand against you."*

This charge of 'having malice in their hearts' is one that featured in most of the prophecies against the neighbouring nations of Judah. They had not merely observed the desolation of the towns and villages of Judah but they had actually come into the land and joined in looting. The presence of foreigners worshipping other gods was regarded as defiling the land belonging to Yahweh.

12 A PROPHECY AGAINST RABBAH Ezekiel 25: 5-7

"I will turn Rabbah into a pasture for camels and Ammon into a resting place for sheep. Then you will know that I am the Lord for this is what the Sovereign Lord says: because you have clapped your hands and stamped your feet, rejoicing with all the malice of your heart against the land of Israel, therefore I will stretch out my hand against you."

At the time Ezekiel wrote these lines which was just after the destruction of Jerusalem in 586, the anger against Ammon was intense. They had not only joined the Babylonian army attacking Judah back in 598, but they had joined Zedekiah's conspiracy in 593 to revolt against Babylon and then failed to come to the aid of Judah when Nebuchadnezzar attacked in 588. We have already noted this, but in addition to breaking their promised support of Jerusalem, the Ammonites gleefully participated in looting the city.

We have already studied the report in Ezekiel 21 where Nebuchadnezzar stopped at the crossroads to consult his gods on whether he should first attack Jerusalem or 'Rabbah of the Ammonites'. Ezekiel reports that God guided the hand of Nebuchadnezzar to go to Jerusalem, but several years later the Babylonians launched a devastating attack upon Ammon from which the Ammonites never really recovered, leaving Rabbah in ruins and the country was occupied by wandering Arab tribes from the east for the next 400 years.

The Ammonites had occupied the territory to the east of the River Jordan for centuries before the people of Israel occupied Canaan. Under Moses' leadership they had passed through Ammon (today's Jordan) but far from being welcomed they were denied food and water. They had even hired Balaam to pronounce a curse upon them. God had turned Balaam's curse into a blessing, but this did not result in a friendship between Ammon and Israel. There was always tension between the two nations. In fact, the Israelites were told, *"Do not seek a treaty of friendship with them as long as you live."* (Deut 23:6).

The Ammonites not only rejoiced openly at the destruction of Jerusalem in 586, but they continued to take advantage of Judah's misfortune by occupying some of the land and infiltrating the remnant of Judah left by the Babylonians. In Jeremiah chapters 40 to 44 there is a detailed account of what happened in the aftermath of the destruction of Jerusalem when the Babylonians appointed Gedaliah as Governor of the province. He made his administrative centre at Mizpah where he was joined by Jeremiah and many of the remaining leaders of Judah, including some army officers, together with men women and children from among the poorest of the land who had not been taken into exile in Babylon.

Gedaliah took an oath to protect them saying, *"Do not be afraid to serve the Babylonians. Settle down in the land and serve the king of Babylon, and it will go well with you."* (Jer 40:9). They did this for some time and they were able to harvest wine, summer fruit and the produce of the land and this attracted a large number of Jews from *"Moab, Ammon, Edom and all the other countries around Judah"* who came to join them (Jer 40:12).

It was at this point that Baalis, King of the Ammonites, sent Ishmael to assassinate Gedaliah. Gedaliah had been warned but he refused to take the report seriously and he warmly entertained Ishmael and the 10 men with him. Whilst they were eating a meal they fell upon Gedaliah, murdering him and killing all the Jews with him and the Babylonian soldiers. This act of treachery significantly changed the history of Judah because it unsettled all those who had come to Mizpah and were settling in under Gedaliah's leadership.

The remnant at Mizpah feared the retribution of Babylon and they approached Jeremiah seeking a word from the Lord on whether or not they should go to seek refuge in Egypt. Facing such an important decision Jeremiah took ten days to seek the Lord but when he gave them the word that they should remain in Judah and not be afraid of the Babylonians, they refused to accept it as a genuine word from God – even accusing him of lying.

Jeremiah brought a further word, *"If you are determined to go to Egypt and you do go to settle there, then the sword you fear will overtake you there, and the famine you dread will follow you into Egypt, and there you will die. Indeed, all who are determined to go to Egypt to settle there will die by the sword, famine, and plague, not one of them will survive or escape the disaster I will bring on them. This is what the Lord Almighty, the God of Israel says."* (Jer 42:15-16)

13 A PROPHECY AGAINST MOAB Ezekiel 25: 8-11

This is what the Sovereign Lord says: "Because Moab and Seir said, "Look the house of Judah has become like all the other nations," therefore I will expose the flank of Moab, beginning at its frontier towns – Beth Jeshimoth, Baal Meon and Kiriathaim – the glory of that land. I will give Moab along with the Ammonites to the people of the east as a possession, so that the Ammonites will not be remembered among the nations, and I will inflict punishment on Moab. Then they will know that I am the Lord.

Ezekiel's strong invective against Moab comes as no surprise because there had been centuries of hostility between Israel and the people of Moab and Ammon, both of whom came from the same root. Their history goes back to the time of Abraham and Lot. According to the account in Genesis 19, Lot had a divine warning that Sodom and Gomorrah were going to be destroyed and that he and all his relatives should leave immediately. Lot spoke to his two sons-in-law who were pledged to marry his daughters telling them to hurry up and get out of the city. They refused to leave and so they lost their lives leaving the two daughters with no prospects of husbands. The girls got their father drunk and used him to become pregnant. The older daughter became the mother of Moab who became the father of the Moabites, and the younger daughter's son became the father of the Ammonites. (Gen 19:36-38)

Both the Moabites and the Ammonites were known as aggressive people and so the Israelites skirted round their territory in their journey from Egypt to Canaan. They occupied the territory east of the Dead Sea between Ammon on the north and parts of Edom to the south. Relationships between Moab and Israel varied from year to year from the time of the Judges to the early years of the monarchy.

At the time of Naomi and her husband Elimelech, there was a famine in the land around Bethlehem, so they and their two sons went to live in Moab. Clearly they were made welcome and they lived there for some years until after the death of Elimelech. Naomi then returned to Bethlehem with one of her daughters in law, Ruth a Moabitess who married Boaz. She became the mother of Jesse who became the father of King David.

The fact that David's grandmother came from Moab certainly did not make David kindly disposed towards Moab. It was David who ruthlessly subdued the Moabites. The exploits of David recorded in 2 Samuel 8 make horrific reading recording that he took a great deal of plunder from Moab, Edom, and the Ammonites. David's policy was followed by his son Solomon who extended his empire as far aast as the River Euphrates. Moab and all the surrounding nations paid tribute to Solomon whose wealth was enormous, but Solomon did not obey the command not to marry women of the Gentile nations. One of his wives was from Moab and *"On a hill east of Jerusalem, Solomon built a high place for Chemosh the detestable God of Moab, and for Molech the detestable God of the Ammonites. He did the same for all his foreign wives"* (1 Kgs 11:7-8).

Amos in 8th century Israel refers to the aggression of Moab. He hears God saying, *"For three sins of Moab, even for four, I will not turn back my wrath, because he burned, as if to lime, the bones of Edom's King. I will send fire upon Moab"* (Amos 2:1-2). Isaiah of Jerusalem, also in the 8th century, spoke an oracle against Moab in which he foresaw the nation suffering a major disaster. Some 200 years later Jeremiah devoted a whole chapter of 47 verses to a dirge about Moab in which he saw, *"The destroyer will come against every town, and not a town will escape"* (Jer 48:8).

Ezekiel's lament follows the destruction of Jerusalem when the Moabites had rejoiced at the suffering of the people of Judah. Moabites had come in and annexed parts of the countryside of Judah which is what is referred to in the reading today as *"exposing the flank of Moab"* and extending its frontier towns. Israel had become just like the other nations with mixed populations. This was true – much to the anger of Ezra and Nehemiah! (Ezra 10:1-4) Nehemiah found that a number of men who had returned from the exile had married women from Ashdod, Ammon and Moab and their children could not even speak the language of Judah (Neh 13:23 -24). This is the background to Ezekiel's Oracle against Moab. He no doubt already knew a lot of what had happened in Jerusalem and what was happening in Judah where the Moabites had already illegally annexed some of the land.

14 A PROPHECY AGAINST EDOM Ezekiel 25:12-14

This is what the Sovereign Lord says: "Because Edom took revenge on the house of Judah and became very guilty by doing so, therefore this is what the Sovereign Lord says: I will stretch out my hand against Edom and kill its men and their animals. I will lay it waste, and from Teman to Dedan they will fall by the sword. I will take vengeance on Edom by the hand of my people Israel and they will deal with Edom in accordance with my anger and my wrath, they will know my vengeance," declares the Sovereign Lord.

Edom was just South of Moab and stretched across the southern boundaries of Judah encompassing much of the Negev and the region known as Mount Seir and reaching South right down below Mount Sinai to the Red Sea. The boundaries with Judah were always a matter of dispute and the tension between Edom and Judah stretched over many centuries. When the people of Israel were leaving Egypt, travelling towards Canaan they were refused entry to the territory of Edom. When Moses sent messengers requesting permission to pass through their territory, *"Edom answered: you may not pass through here; if you try, we will march out and attack you with the sword."* Israel made a promise only to pass along the main road and not to stray either side, but still their request was refused and Israel had to find another route (Num 20:18-20).

The intense hatred between Edom and Judah can only be understood in the context of the origins of the two people-groups. For this, we have to go back to Genesis 25:21-34. Rebecca was the mother of twins – Esau and Jacob. Esau (or Edom – the hairy one) was the firstborn and Jacob (the deceiver) was the second child. Rebecca was said to have received a word from the Lord that two nations were in her womb and that the older would serve the younger (Gen 25:23). Esau was said to have sold his birthright when he was hungry, for some bread and a pot of stew. The tension between the two men grew throughout their lives and was inherited by their descendants.

The worst period of conflict between the two nations appears to have been in the time of King David's reign. It is reported, *"David became famous after he returned from striking down 18,000 Edomites in the Valley of Salt. He put garrisons throughout Edom, and all the Edomites became subject to David. The Lord gave David victory wherever he went"* (2 Sam 8:13-14).

It is events such as this that intensified the hatred of the Edomites for the people of Judah. The domination of Edom was continued under the reign of King Solomon and to some extent by his successors. This established a sense of oppression among the people of Edom and a deep resentment of the power of domination over them exercised by Judah. This stretched back to what they saw as the great deception that had been inflicted upon them by their ancestors, from which they continued to suffer for hundreds of years.

This is the background to relationships between the two nations that was existing right up to the time of King Zedekiah when Edom decided to cooperate in the proposed conspiracy to revolt against Babylon led by Egypt and King Zedekiah in 593 (Jer 27). Zedekiah went ahead with his revolt but none of the other nations did so, leaving Judah to take the full onslaught from Babylon. Edom's traditional hatred of Judah then caused them to rejoice in Judah's misfortune and this is what lay behind Ezekiel's lament and his statement *"Edom took revenge on the house of Judah and became very guilty by doing so."*

It is unsurprising that Ezekiel follows this statement by saying that God would take vengeance upon Edom by the hand of the people of Judah whom he describes as *"my people Israel".* This would no doubt come as a great encouragement to the people in exile in Babylon, that God still regarded them as '*his people*'. This would be understood as saying that God regarded them as being within the covenant that he made at Sinai and that he would therefore watch over them with all the blessings listed in Deuteronomy 28:1-14.

This was fulfilling the ministry that God had called Ezekiel to carry out that would prepare the people of Israel in exile to return to the land as a redeemed company of believers, cleansed from all the spiritual contamination of idolatry. They would be a people whose total loyalty was to Yahweh the God of Israel. They would return to the land and rebuild Jerusalem and their trust would be totally in God, and in him alone.

15 A PROPHECY AGAINST PHILISTIA
Ezekiel 25:15-17

This is what the Sovereign Lord says: "Because the Philistines acted in vengeance and took revenge with malice in their hearts, and with ancient hostility sought to destroy Judah, therefore this is what the Sovereign Lord says: 'I am about to stretch out my hand against the Philistines, and I will cut off the Kerethites and destroy those remaining along the coast' . . ."

The first mention of Philistia in the Bible is in Exodus 13:17 when the people of Israel had just escaped from Egypt, but Moses received a divine instruction not to lead the people northward along the coastal path through the territory of the Philistines where they would undoubtedly have faced a well-armed army for which they were in no way prepared. The first record of meeting the Philistines is in the period of the Judges, in the early days of the settlement in Canaan, in the time of Eli the priest and the early days of the prophet Samuel.

Gaza, Ashdod, and Ashkelon had been Philistine territory for centuries and there had been constant incursions in an easterly direction into land occupied by the Canaanites. When the Israelites settled among the Canaanites they faced constant surprise attacks upon the their villages when men women and children were randomly killed. The exploits of some of the Israelite heroes such as Samson show attempts to deal with these incursions. Throughout the period of the Judges the Israelites were constantly at a disadvantage because they were only armed with wooden weapons such as staves.

There is a revealing note in 1 Samuel 13:19 showing the lack of social organisation among the Israelites. *"Not a blacksmith could be found in the whole land of Israel because the Philistines had said, 'otherwise the Hebrews will make swords or spears!' So all Israel went down to the Philistines to have their ploughshares, mattocks, axes and sickles sharpened."* A further note shows the lack of preparations for defence: *"So on the day of the battle not a soldier with Saul and Jonathan had a sword or spear in his hand; only Saul and his son Jonathan had them"* (1 Sam 13:22).

The Philistines loved fighting and they famously had bands of mercenaries called Kerethites (or Cherethites) who hired themselves out to other nations to fight in their wars. Amazingly, King David used them in some of his battles and then hired them for his ceremonial palace guard in Jerusalem!

King David did a lot to subdue them but it was not until the reign of Solomon that the Philistines were really subdued. Solomon's Empire stretched from the borders of Egypt in the south to Lebanon in the north, and from the Mediterranean in the west to the River Euphrates in the east, but his son Rehoboam was an incompetent leader whose foolishness led to the division of the land into Israel in the north and Judah in the south.

Then in the 8th century came war between the Assyrians and the Egyptians which is referred to by Isaiah. *"In the year that the supreme commander, sent by Sargon King of Assyria, came to Ashdod and attacked and captured it – at that time the Lord spoke through Isaiah son of Amoz"* (Is 20:1). This led to Isaiah stripping and going barefoot around Jerusalem, warning that this would be the fate of all those who put their trust in Egypt.

The Assyrians also attacked Jerusalem, sending a threatening message saying that none of the gods of other nations had been able to stand against them so why did they trust the God of Israel? Isaiah and King Hezekiah spread the letter before the Lord in the temple and prayed together. *"Then the angel of the Lord went out and put to death 185,000 men in the Assyrian camp"* (Is 37:36).

The rise of Babylon and the downfall of the Assyrians brought a further attack upon the Philistines on the coastal highway when the Babylonians made an unsuccessful attempt to attack Egypt. Gaza, Ashdod, and Ashkelon as coastal towns on the main highway constantly suffered from the hostility between Babylon and Egypt.

When the Babylonians attacked Jerusalem in 588 and began a two-year siege they also carried out widescale destruction right across Judah. The Philistines took advantage, and with the countryside of Judah left unguarded and major towns destroyed, they were free to take control of large areas. They also went across to the ruins of Jerusalem looting and rejoicing, with *"malice in their hearts, and with ancient hostility"* according to Ezekiel's lament. This was why the Lord said that he would *"carry out great vengeance on them and punish them in my wrath."*

16 NEBUCHADNEZZAR TO DESTROY TYRE
Ezekiel 26:1-14

In the eleventh year, on the first day of the month, the word of the Lord came to me: "Son of man, because Tyre has said of Jerusalem, 'Aha! The gate to the nations is broken, and its doors have swung open to me; now that she lies in ruins I will prosper,' therefore this is what the Sovereign Lord says: 'I am against you, O Tyre, and I will bring many nations against you, like the sea casting up its waves' . . ."

In Ezekiel 26 there is an amalgam of four oracles each with their introductory formula and ending. We are dealing with the first two oracles in the first half of the chapter, verses 1-6 and 7-14. They foresee a time of tremendous slaughter of the population of Tyre and its surrounding area that will plunder the wealth of the Phoenicians and destroy their trading empire. This great destruction would be carried out by Nebuchadnezzar as part of the Babylonian Empire moving westward to occupy part of the Mediterranean coast. Babylon had designs of taking a share of the enormous wealth being generated in Lebanon by the coastal cities of the Phoenicians and their trading empire across the Mediterranean world.

Tyre, the capital city of the Phoenicians has an amazing history. The ancient city on the Mediterranean coast of what is now Lebanon was fortified by a giant causeway built out from the mainland to connect it to a small rocky island which then became an impregnable fortress able to withstand the onslaught of invaders. Nebuchadnezzar laid siege to Tyre for some 13 years and he still did not conquer it. The city's wealth was furnished largely from its extensive seaborne trade, exporting purple dye extracted from shellfish along the coast. It also acted as a port for the Phoenicians who travelled extensively, even setting up trading posts as far away as Cornwall and the Isle of Wight.

The Phoenicians reached a peak of their power under Hiram whose tomb, a massive limestone sarcophagus can still be seen about 6 miles south of Tyre. He was succeeded by his son Ethbaal whose daughter was Jezebel who married Ahab the king of the northern kingdom of Israel. She took with her many of her priests and established the worship of the Tyrian Baal in Israel which was strongly opposed by the Prophet Elijah. The extent to which Jezebel was successful in establishing her religion in Israel is recorded in the words of Elijah who said, *"I am the only one of the Lord's prophets left, but Baal has 450 prophets"* (1 Kgs 18:22).

Elijah's confrontation with the priests of Baal on Mount Carmel is recorded in 1 Kings 18 where he challenged the priests of Baal to call down fire from their God to burn up the sacrifice on the altar. When they were unable to do this Elijah poured water on the wood and called upon Yahweh, the God of Israe, who sent fire that burned up the sacrifice. Then Elijah presided over the killing of all the priests of Baal (1 Kgs 18:40). This was bitterly resented by the people of Tyre who saw the killing of their priests as the violation of their princess Jezebel and a direct insult to the King of Tyre.

That confrontation between Elijah and Jezebel was strongly influential in forming the social and political relationships between Israel and Tyre. The slaughtering of the priests of Tyre was seen as an act of war, after which hostility towards Israel lasted for centuries. When Jerusalem was sacked by the Babylonians in 586 the population of Tyre rejoiced which is reflected in the opening words of the passage we are studying today. Both Tyre and the Phoenician trading posts or settlements along the Mediterranean coast were prophesied to be destroyed by the Babylonians. Jeremiah regarded Nebuchadnezzar as God's instrument of justice destined to rule the whole region (Jer 27:7).

Tyre had been forced by Sennacherib to pay tribute to the Assyrians and this was deeply resented, so they rejoiced when Babylon was victorious at the Battle of Carchemish in 605, but they discovered that the Babylonians were just as aggressive as the Assyrians. It was no doubt for this reason that they joined in the conspiracy with Sidon, Judah, Edom, Moab, and Ammon in 593 to revolt against Nebuchadnezzar. Just shortly after this, Egypt got into the act in 588 by attacking Tyre and Sidon to secure their help against Babylon. This brought Nebuchadnezzar back into the area with his 13 years' siege of Tyre, from 586 to 573. It was during this time of siege that Ezekiel's lament was written, foreseeing the plundering of the wealth of Tyre's trading empire across the Mediterranean world.

17 THE COASTLANDS WILL TREMBLE
Ezekiel 26:15-21

This is what the Sovereign Lord says to Tyre: "Will not the coastlands tremble at the sound of your fall, when the wounded groan and the slaughter takes place in you? Then all the princes of the coast will step down from their thrones and lay aside their robes and take off their embroidered garments. . . . When I bring the ocean depths over you and its vast waters cover you, then I will bring you down with those who go down to the pit . . ."

In the second half of chapter 26 we are dealing with the final two oracles, verses 15-18 and verses 19-21. They each form a small unit of lament with their own introductory formula. The first oracle concludes with a short lament in verses 17-18 in the form of a song which no doubt would have made it easily remembered for those listening to Ezekiel. We know that he was a musician and that he had a beautiful voice, so this would have made his lament all the more memorable.

Verse 15 begins with the declaration that the coastlands will tremble. The coastlands of Lebanon around Tyre were the primary source of wealth that had been accumulated over centuries of trading. It had begun with producing a purple dye from the local shellfish, the secrets of which were strongly guarded. The reference to the 'princes of the coast' is a description of the wealthy merchants who controlled the coastlands area of Lebanon.

These 'princes' or rulers behaved like warlords with private armies and vast navies of trading ships. Their skilled sailors went to ports all across the Mediterranean with trading colonies in Malta, Sicily, Sardinia, Marseille, and Spain. They even ventured into the Atlantic and crossed the notorious Bay of Biscay to reach England, trading in gold, silver, and tin. The tin mines of Cornwall, and a trading post on the Isle of Wight, were known to be important bases of the Phoenician fleet. In a prophecy about Tyre, Isaiah speaks of the merchants of Sidon whom the seafarers have enriched as the 'marketplace of the world' (Is 23:2-3).

Ezekiel prophesied that this whole trading empire would collapse and *"the princes of the coast will step down from their thrones and lay aside their robes."* They sit on the ground trembling and appalled at the disaster that has befallen them. They do not tear their robes as was the customary practice. Their embroidered garments were too precious to tear to pieces as Job's friends did when they came to comfort him and *"they sat on the ground with him for seven days and seven nights"* (Job 2:13).

According to Ezekiel's prophecy, the rulers of Tyre and all the places along the coast of Lebanon would be appalled at the collapse of their empire. In the final part of chapter 26, verses 19-21, there is an oracle of the desolation that is coming upon the cities of Lebanon. The depths of the ocean will sweep over the coastal cities and make them desolate. *"Then I will bring you down with those who go down to the pit, to the people of long ago."*

This is an amalgam of verses from chapters 31 and 32 where there are further laments of what God is going to do to the people of Lebanon in taking the people down to the grave. This is all said to be the direct action of the Sovereign Lord. *"I will make you dwell in the earth below, as in ancient ruins, with those who go down to the pit."*

This is followed by the final pronunciation against the city, which is said to become desolate and no longer inhabited, with its population thrown into the underworld with no possibility of a return from Hades to the land of the living. The Phoenician people with all their trading wealth and influence will simply be wiped out of existence so that they will be left without a trace.

This devastating judgement upon Tyre is also foreseen by Amos back in the 8th century, *"because she sold whole communities of captives to Edom disregarding a treaty of brotherhood, I will send fire upon the walls of Tyre that will consume her fortresses"* (Amos 1:9-10). The reputation of the Phoenician people for cruelty was legendary and Ezekiel foresees God himself bringing judgement upon them and taking Tyre down into Hades from which there would be no return. This is an interesting glimpse into current understanding of life after death in the time of Ezekiel. He sees the people of Tyre going down into Hades where they meet with people who had been cast there from ancient ruins. This would be *"a horrible end and you will be no more"* which indicated belief that those who came under the judgement of God would have no afterlife.

18 A LAMENT FOR TYRE Ezekiel 27: 1-11

The word of the Lord came to me: "Son of man, take up a lament concerning Tyre. Say to Tyre, situated at the gateway to the sea, merchant of peoples on many coasts, 'This is what the Sovereign Lord says: "You say, O Tyre, I am perfect in beauty. Your domain was on the high seas; your builders brought your beauty to perfection. They made all your timbers of pine trees from Senir, they took a cedar from Lebanon to make a mast for you, of oaks from Bashan they made your oars; of cypress wood from the coast of Cyprus they made your deck, inlaid with ivory"' . . ."

Chapter 27 begins with the usual introduction. There follows a lament about Tyre that is a lengthy poem in two parts which are separated by a piece of prose running from verses 12-24. The prose is of considerable interest as an historical account of commerce in the 6th century BC. It lists many of the places that the Phoenicians reached through their trading empire that stretched from the eastern shores of the Mediterranean through to the Atlantic Ocean and the English Channel where the Phoenicians established a settlement in Cornwall, trading in tin from the Cornish mines. They also established another trading post on the Isle of Wight.

Verse 17 is of particular interest in listing Judah and Israel as trading with Tyre. This trade agreement goes back to the time of King David who expanded the territory of Israel to cover much of Lebanon, probably more than 10 miles north of Tyre and Sidon. David's kingdom stretched across parts of Syria and Ammon in the east and south down the Mediterranean coast as far as Philistine territory and inland stretching south to the wilderness beyond Beersheba. This meant that David controlled the main caravan routes from the east to the Mediterranean coast and therefore a deal with Tyre would be mutually beneficial. They made a treaty in 968.

There is an interesting background to this recorded in 2 Samuel 5:9-12 which is worth recording here. *"David then took up residence in the fortress and called it the City of David. He built up the area around it, from the supporting terraces inward. And he became more and more powerful, because the Lord God Almighty was with him. Now Hiram King of Tyre sent messengers to David, along with cedar logs and carpenters and stonemasons, and they built a palace for David."* This was an incredibly generous gift marking David's acquisition of Jerusalem and establishing it as his new national capital. Tyre was renowned for its skilled craftsman as well as its wealth and vast quantities of wood. As a sea power Tyre's empire was virtually unassailable by any other marine state, but on land it was always vulnerable and to have David as a friendly neighbour having power on his borders and being able to protect the trade routes was an enormous advantage to Hiram. Hence, he made a trade deal with David and this was carried over into the era of David's son Solomon.

The whole of 1 Kings 5 is of considerable interest as the background to relationships between Tyre and Israel during Solomon's reign. Hiram and David certainly had a close personal relationship and friendship, but although the trading arrangement continued into Solomon's reign it was on a purely commercial basis and Solomon agreed to give an enormous amount of wheat and olive oil in return for the materials and expert labour supplied by Tyre (1 Kgs 5:10-11).

We have already referred to the marriage of Jezebel to Ahab, king of the northern kingdom of Israel, who introduced her gods to Israel bringing many of her priests with her to establish the practice of her Baal worship in the land. This was a regular practice in those days, of nations cementing friendly relationships by recognising each other's gods. The prophetic tradition of Israel prevented this and stood against any treaty obligations with other nations, seeing this as treachery to Yahweh the God of Israel. This is an important factor in determining relationships between Israel and Judah on the one hand and neighbouring nations, as well as with the major powers of Assyria, Babylon, and Egypt.

The warm relationship between Tyre and Israel was shattered by the Prophet Elijah slaughtering Jezebel's priests. So in the poem that forms the major part of Ezekiel 27 that covers 3-11 and resumes at 27:25, we see a lament for the demise of Tyre that is represented as a great shipwreck in 27:27, the news of which went around the coasts where the Phoenicians traded and where they acquired their wealth. *"All who live in the coastlands are appalled at you."* The next chapter resumes this theme and gives an explanation.

19 THE PROUD KING OF TYRE Ezekiel 28:1-19

The word of the Lord came to me: "Son of man, say to the ruler of Tyre, this is what the Sovereign Lord says: 'In the pride of your heart you say, I am a god; I sit on the throne of a god in the heart of the seas.' But you are a man and not a god though you think you are as wise as a god."

Ezekiel 28 continues the theme of the previous chapter coming from the time of the Babylonian siege of Tyre which lasted for 13 years from 586 to 573. The lament in this chapter was near the end of the siege around the year 576. It is included here by the scribes of Ezekiel's school who recorded his ministry.

This poetic account of the great pride, wisdom, skill, and wealth acquired by the King of Tyre who lived in a paradise of perfection has parallels with the account of Adam and Eve in the Garden of Eden. In chapter 27 we read of the perfection of beauty (27:3-4) and here we see all the perfection personified into one man – the ruler of Tyre as Ezekiel 28:14-15 uses the Genesis creation story of the fall of mankind. Hiram had acquired wisdom and understanding as well as wealth and began to think of himself as wise as God, in the same way as Adam and Eve had eaten from the fruit of the tree of life and acquired wisdom so that they could be like God (Gen 3:5).

The judgement upon the king who represents the people of Tyre begins at verse 6 where we see their great pride, thinking themselves as gods who rule the world. Their ships sailed everywhere, and all nations did obeisance to them. A foreign army of ruthless warriors would descend upon them. "*They will bring you down to the pit, and you will die a violent death in the heart of the seas*" (28:8).

Ezekiel would have known that Nebuchadnezzar was laying siege to Tyre at the time of composing this poem. The Babylonians were working out their anger and revenge upon those who had joined in the conspiracy initiated by Zedekiah at a meeting in Jerusalem in 593, recorded in Jeremiah 27:3. The pride and arrogance of Tyre and their absolute disregard for the rights of humanity or even of keeping agreements with other nations was legendary. Amos, the 8th century prophet, refers to this, "*For three sins of Tyre, even for four,*

I will not turn back my wrath because she sold whole communities of captives to Edom, disregarding a treaty of brotherhood" (Amos 1:9).

The 13 year siege of Tyre by the Babylonians was eventually resolved by 573 on terms agreed by both sides, but it had had a devastating effect upon Tyre's commercial activities that resulted in 50 years of poverty when they struggled to regain their dominance of the seas and their trade with their many settlements and trading posts. Ezekiel had prophesied Nebuchadnezzar's invasion saying that *"He will ravage your settlements on the mainland with the sword; he will set up siege works against you"* (26:7-8).

We know that Tyre did recover much of its trade after the end of the siege because Nehemiah visited Jerusalem about the year 440 when he said, *"Men from Tyre who lived in Jerusalem were bringing in fish and all kinds of merchandise and selling them in Jerusalem on the Sabbath to the people of Judah"* (Neh 13:16). Artaxerxes III sacked Sidon in 332, but by far the worst time of bloodshed was when Alexander the Great began his movement east to extend his empire. He arrived on the mainland of Tyre and requested to go across onto the island fortress to worship in the temple of Melkarth whom Alexander worshiped. His request was refused and led to his laying siege to the island fortress. He destroyed the old town of Tyre and used the rubble to fill the gap between the mainland and the island. Still unable to breach their defences, he raised a fleet of 224 ships and invaded by sea. He then wreaked terrible revenge by killing 8000, crucifying 2000 on the beach and selling 30,000 into slavery.

By New Testament times both Tyre and Sidon had recovered, and they welcomed Jesus (Mark 7:24-30). In Apostolic times there was a Christian church in Tyre. Luke records Paul's visit to Tyre saying, *"Finding the disciples there, we stayed with them seven days. Through the Spirit they urged Paul not to go on to Jerusalem."* (Acts 21:4-5). Church history shows Origen escaping the Bishop of Alexandria and finding safe shelter in Tyre where he stayed, ministering there for many years until the end of his life.

20 JUDGEMENT UPON SIDON Ezekiel 28:20-26

The word of the Lord came to me: "Son of man, set your face against Sidon; prophesy against her and say: this is what the Sovereign Lord says: 'I am against you, O Sidon, and I will gain glory within you. They will know that I am the Lord, when I inflict punishment on her and show myself holy within her' . . ."

This prophecy against Sidon is part of the invective against Tyre that has occupied the whole of chapters 26 and 27 and the first part of chapter 28. Tyre and Sidon were closely connected, not only geographically but culturally and economically. Together they were part of the Phoenician Empire that spread across the Mediterranean and as far west as Cornwall and the Isle of Wight. The Phoenician base at Carthage on the north coast of Africa was unrivalled in economic power in the region.

The wealth generated by the trade of Tyre and Sidon was renowned throughout the world but was also known for its violence and oppression. It was feared throughout the region. "*Through your widespread trade you were filled with violence, and you sinned. So I drove you in disgrace from the Mount of God*" (28:16). This is thought to be a reference to the time when both Tyre and Sidon had sent representatives to Jerusalem at the invitation of Zedekiah to consider joining a revolt against Babylon to be led by Egypt. We have already dealt with this and noted Jeremiah's strong opposition (Jer 27).

Both Tyre and Sidon had agreed to be part of the conspiracy against Babylon, and this had brought an angry reaction from Nebuchadnezzar. Following the destruction of Jerusalem in 586 he turned his attention to the smaller states around Judah to deliver punishment to each of them. We have already noted that Nebuchadnezzar engaged in a long siege against Tyre that lasted for 13 years and caused enormous suffering within the city. The Babylonian soldiers were also severely distressed from the long campaign and eventually terms were agreed that satisfied both parties.

The fate of Sidon was sealed much earlier. They surrendered almost immediately because of a plague that swept through the population of the city. This was prophesied by Ezekiel who foresaw the siege against the city that Nebuchadnezzar would set. *"I will send a plague upon her and make blood flow in her streets. The slain will fall within her, with the sword against her on every side, then they will know that I am the Lord"* (28:23). Ezekiel saw this plague as coming from the hand of God because the people of Tyre and Sidon did not fulfil their promised support to Zedekiah. They not only failed to support Jerusalem when the city was attacked, but they actually rejoiced in the destruction of Jerusalem carried out by the Babylonians.

Both Tyre and Sidon were totally committed to the acquisition of wealth and the pursuit of economic power right across their Empire, and they greatly coveted the trade group that ran across the land of Israel from north to south, from Lebanon and Syria to Egypt. Jerusalem was an important trading post and the Phoenicians greatly coveted the opportunity that was presented to them by Nebuchadnezzar's invasion of Judah and the destruction of Jerusalem. They eagerly stepped into the economic breach in the trade route. Ezekiel 28:24 provides the clue for Ezekiel's invective against Sidon: *"No longer will the people of Israel have malicious neighbours who are painful briars and sharp thorns. Then they will know that I am the Sovereign Lord."*

The Phoenician merchants gladly took over the trade that ran through Jerusalem thus increasing the pain and distress of the city and its humiliation in the eyes of all the surrounding nations. They were indeed 'painful briars and sharp thorns', adding to the suffering of the people of Israel. Ezekiel sees this as a reason for God to bring judgement upon the people of Tyre and Sidon and he looks forward to the 'Day of the Lord' when God would punish those who had increased the distress of his people in their hour of need.

Ezekiel uses this to look forward to the end of the exile when God would fulfil his promise to return the exiles to the land of Israel when they will rebuild the economy and live in safety. He sees this as a time when God would reveal his nature and purposes to the Gentile nations through exercising his power to restore his people. This would demonstrate, not only the Sovereignty of God as the Lord of history who holds all nations in his hands, but it would show his justice and his holiness in contrast to the values of the world which are based upon wealth and power and oppression.

21 ORACLES[3] AGAINST EGYPT Ezekiel 29

In the tenth year, in the tenth month on the twelfth day, the word of the Lord came to me: "Son of man set your face against Pharaoh king of Egypt and prophesy against him and against all Egypt."

The background to Ezekiel 29 which is dated January 587, just one year before the destruction of Jerusalem shows that it was written in the second year of the Babylonian siege of Jerusalem. Both Jeremiah and Ezekiel regarded Nebuchadnezzar as an instrument in the hands of God to execute judgement upon unrighteousness. He was raised up for this purpose and thus was a servant of Yahweh. The Babylonians had crushed the Egyptian army at Carchemish in 605 before moving against Judah. Jerusalem had surrendered in 598 when Nebuchadnezzar had appointed Zedekiah to replace Jehoiachin making him swear in the name of Yahweh the God of Israel, an oath of loyalty to Babylon.

Ezekiel is reflecting the strong anti-Egypt sentiment in Judah, where there was a tremendous sense of bitterness because Egypt was largely seen as the cause for the siege that now imprisoned Jerusalem. Egypt and Babylon were the two major powers who were constantly vying for control of the whole region. Egypt had been stirring up anti-Babylonian sentiment in Israel and the surrounding nations. They had incited Zedekiah to revolt against Babylon with the promise of armed support and this had resulted in the conspiracy recorded in Jeremiah 27 where representatives from Edom, Moab, Ammon, Tyre and Sidon all came to agree a united strategy to break the control Babylon was exercising over the region.

Egypt's promised military support did not materialise when the Babylonians attacked Judah in 588. Zedekiah had gone ahead with his revolt, relying upon Egypt, despite the strong opposition of Jeremiah who regarded Egypt as 'a broken reed'. He said that anyone who relied upon her would be disappointed. Ezekiel repeats this with a descriptive metaphor saying, *"You have been a staff of reed for the*

---

3 The word 'oracle' used here is a divinely inspired story or saying, as in Ezekiel 12:10, and extensively in Isaiah.

house of Israel. When they grasped you with their hands, you splintered and you tore open their shoulders" (Ezek 29:6-7).

Ezekiel 29 consists of four short oracles, each of them directed towards Egypt and Pharaoh king of Egypt, who is described as a river monster or crocodile crouching among the streams waiting for prey. The Hebrew word 'lying' literally is 'crouching' in a menacing posture awaiting the fish. Pharaoh had raised himself up as though he were the creator of the River Nile and he had ultimate authority over it and the wealth that it produced, but he would come under judgement and be removed from his little paradise and there will be no one to save him.

In the second Oracle, 6-12, the focus is on Egypt's treachery by breaking their promise to support Jerusalem if she were attacked. The promise here is that God would bring judgement upon them turning the whole land of Egypt into a desolate wasteland. The phrase *'from Migdol to Aswan'* simply means from one end of the land to the other, like saying from north to south, or from Dan to Beersheba.

The third Oracle, 13-16 says that after a number of years being scattered among the nations, they would come back to their land but that Egypt would be much reduced in size and the people would live in Upper Egypt near the source of the Nile where they would no longer have the great wealth from the River that had been enjoyed in former years. This reduced status of Egypt would be a sign to Israel – a reminder of their sin in not putting their trust in Yahweh, but in looking to Egypt for support.

The fourth Oracle was that Nebuchadnezzar would be the means of bringing judgement upon Egypt and his reward would be to plunder the land, much of which would be given as loot to his army as a reward for all that they had done in Tyre and Sidon as well as in Egypt. This fourth and final Oracle was the promise of a horn growing in the house of Israel. The horn was a symbol of strength, and this was foreshadowed in Psalm 132:17 *"Here I will make a horn grow for David and set up a lamp for my anointed one. I will clothe his enemies with shame, but the crown on his head shall be resplendent."*

Judah would go back to the land and rebuild Jerusalem and the temple. Here Ezekiel was reflecting the growing belief that God will raise up someone from the line of David, their ideal King, to lead the rebuilding of the nation and ensure its prosperity. This may be an early reflection of the Messianic hope of Israel.

22 A LAMENT FOR EGYPT Ezekiel 30:1-19

The word of the Lord came to me: "Son of man, prophesy and say: This is what the Sovereign Lord says: 'Wail and say, alas for that day! For the day is near, the day of the Lord is near – a day of clouds, a time of doom for the nations' . . ."

Ezekiel 30 continues the theme of the previous chapter that we have been examining with its four oracles all directed against Egypt. In this passage we have three oracles, the first is in verses 2-8, the second in 10-12, and the third in 13-19.

As noted in the Introduction, our basic approach to the study of the Bible is to search for the historical background. It would not be possible to understand the message in this chapter without knowing what was happening at this time. The date is given in verse 20 which we will cover in the next study, but it is essential to note here for the whole of chapter 30. It was the 11th year of the exile, day seven of the first month, which was April 587.

The Babylonian army had reached Jerusalem in 588 and begun their siege of that city. They had been surrounding the city for about a year which was creating conditions of famine and extreme hardship among the people inside the city. At about this time news reached the Babylonians that the Egyptian army had just left Egypt, heading for Judah to give support to Zedekiah's revolt as they had agreed when the conspiracy with neighbouring nations had been formed which was strongly opposed by Jeremiah (Jer 27).

At this time, noted in Jeremiah 34, the Babylonians withdrew from their siege of Jerusalem and went to face the army of Egypt. This was something that Hophra and his predecessor had incited. The coalition of small states had all come to Jerusalem as recorded in Jeremiah 27:3. They all had reason to hate the Babylonians and were happy to join the Egyptians in a concerted effort to rid the region of Babylonian control. None of them, however, actually came to the aid of Judah, and the Egyptian intervention came to nothing as Jeremiah had warned that it would.

The Egyptians reached the outskirts of Judah but there is no record of a battle being fought. The Egyptians evidently turned around and ran home leaving Zedekiah alone to face the wrath of Nebuchadnezzar. This was tragic for the people of Judah because the Babylonian army spread right across the countryside slaughtering the population, setting fire to villages and towns in a scorched earth campaign.

The lifting of the siege was greeted with joy inside Jerusalem. The wealthy citizens had set their slaves free so they would not have to feed them, but when the siege was lifted, *"they changed their minds and took back the slaves they had freed and enslaved them again"* (Jer 34:11). This infuriated Jeremiah who quoted, *"You have not proclaimed freedom for your fellow countrymen. So I now proclaim freedom for you, declares the Lord – freedom to fall by the sword, plague and famine"* (Jer 34:17).

Jeremiah went on further to warn that the hopes that Egypt had come to their rescue were utterly false. He was so sure that God had pronounced judgement upon Jerusalem that he said, *"I'm going to give the order, declares the Lord, and I will bring them back to this city . . . And I will lay waste the towns of Judah so that no one can live there"* (Jer 34: 22).

Both Jeremiah and Ezekiel were highly critical of Egypt for breaking their promises. They saw Egypt as largely responsible for the tragedy that befell Judah and the city of Jerusalem hence the fierceness of the oracles against Egypt in this chapter which Ezekiel saw as a day of the Lord in judgement upon Egypt, *"The day of the Lord is near – a day of clouds, a time of doom for the nations. A sword will come against Egypt, and anguish will come upon Cush"* (30:4).

'The Day of the Lord' had traditionally been seen in Israel as a day when God would bring retribution against their enemies. Amos had turned this around as a day of judgement upon Israel itself. It was a day of darkness and not of light (Amos 5:18). Ezekiel, by this time had completely accepted Jeremiah's teaching that Judah had broken the covenant and was now under judgement. He too would have heard that the Egyptians were coming against Babylon but he warned that they and all their allies would fall by the sword. God was saying, *"I will put an end to the hordes of Egypt by the hand of Nebuchadnezzar"* (30:10). This showed the sovereignty of God who held the nations in his hands, *"And they will know that I am the Lord"* (v. 19)

23 BREAKING THE ARM OF PHARAOH
Ezekiel 30:20-29

In the eleventh year, in the first month of the seventh day, the word of the Lord came to me: "Son of man, I have broken the arm of Pharaoh king of Egypt . . . I am against Pharaoh king of Egypt. I will break both his arms."

The whole of chapter 30 is a lament for Egypt which concludes with a piece of prose in verses 20 – 26, dated April 587, one year before the destruction of Jerusalem. We have already examined the first part of the chapter with its strong condemnation of Egypt and the declaration that God was going to use the Babylonians – *"the most ruthless of nations"* – to destroy the land of Egypt (30:11).

In this prose section at the end of chapter 30, Ezekiel begins by recalling the crushing defeat that Egypt had suffered at the hands of the Babylonians at Carchemish in 605. He saw this as God breaking Pharaoh's arm so that he could not hold a sword. The Egyptian army had retreated in tatters and had run for home in the aftermath of the Battle of Carchemish at which the Babylonians had taken on a combined army of Egyptians and Assyrians and had roundly defeated them. Babylon had proved that they were now the mighty empire ruling the region.

Egypt had been humiliated when the remnant of its army reached safety back in Egypt, which Ezekiel sees as a just punishment for the sins of Egypt for all the evil they had done to other nations. That battle had taken place during the reign of the previous Pharaoh. He had been succeeded by Pharaoh Hophra who was a proud man, actually claiming divine power as the incarnation of the god Horus. Hophra's boasting was notorious and he described himself as the 'Possessor of a Strong Arm' who would reverse the humiliation of his predecessor and re-establish the supremacy of Egypt and its satellites in the region.

This is what Ezekiel had referred to in the first and second oracles in this chapter. He had spoken of *"Cush and Put, Lydia and all Arabia, Libya and the people of the covenant land will fall by the sword along with*

Egypt" (30:5). The people of the covenant land were, of course Judah, and Ezekiel had probably already heard that the Babylonians had lifted their siege of Jerusalem and the people of the city were rejoicing. He may even have heard from Jeremiah who had roundly condemned the wealthy citizens who had reclaimed their slaves as soon as the Babylonian army disappeared from outside the walls of Jerusalem.

Ezekiel adds his voice to that of Jeremiah saying that God was going to inflict punishment upon Egypt and that her proud strength will come to an end. Ezekiel saw the flight of the Egyptian army after their defeat at Carchemish as the breaking of Pharaoh's arm, so the man who was claiming to be the possessor of a strong arm had got a broken arm that could not possibly hold a sword. Therefore, it was ridiculous for the people of Jerusalem to hold any hope of Egypt coming to their rescue. Far from God doing a miracle of healing – he was so against Pharaoh Hophra that he would break the other arm. *"I will break both his arms, the good arm as well as the broken one, and make the sword fall from his hand"* (v. 22).

Ezekiel saw the Egyptians fleeing from Judah as the breaking of the other arm leaving Pharaoh powerless. The sword would fall from his hand and both his hands would fall limp. He said: *"I will strengthen the arms of the king of Babylon, but the arms of Pharaoh will fall limp" (v. 25).* Pharaoh would not only be unable to help Judah or save Jerusalem from destruction, but God would put Pharaoh's sword into the hands of Nebuchadnezzar.

All the oracles in this chapter including the final one that we are studying here, are a demonstration of the sovereignty of Yahweh the God of Israel. He not only holds the destiny of the people of Judah in his hands, but he exercises his power over all nations. *"Then they will know that I am the Lord, when I put my sword into the hand of the king of Babylon and he brandishes it against Egypt"* (30:25).

Jeremiah had spoken of this sovereignty of God when the envoys of neighbouring nations came to form the conspiracy against Babylon. He made the extraordinary statement, *"I made the earth and its people and the animals that are on it, and I give it to anyone I please. Now I will hand all your countries over to my servant Nebuchadnezzar king of Babylon"* (Jer 27:5). Ezekiel follows this with God putting a sword into the hands of Babylon.

24 THE TREE OF LIFE Ezekiel 31

In the eleventh year, in the third month on the first day, the word of the Lord came to me: Son of man, say to Pharaoh king of Egypt and to his hordes: "Who can be compared with you in majesty? Consider Assyria, once a cedar in Lebanon . . . it towered on high, its top above the thick foliage."

This chapter is composed of a prophetic poem and two prose pieces which are interpretations of the poem. The poem is in verses 2-9 and the two prose pieces are 10-14 and 15-18. The subject of the poem is 'the tree of life' – an ancient fable that comes from many different sources. There is no introductory formula as is usual in Ezekiel's work although he is told to address this word to, "*Pharaoh king of Egypt and to his hordes.*" This poem is simply introduced with the question "*Who can be compared with you in majesty?*" The question is clearly intended to be irony, although Egypt is not mentioned again until the end of the chapter. The purpose of the poem and its interpretation is directed at the pride and self-adulation of Egypt.

The subject of the poem describing a beautiful tree is a story that everyone would have been familiar with at that time. Different versions were told in different parts of the world and in different traditions, but there is a common link to the world of nature that is represented in a beautiful tree whose roots go down deep into the earth and whose branches reach up high into the sky. The fable clearly has, for some cultures, links to the Garden of Eden and 'the tree of life' in its centre. In the Genesis tradition it is alongside 'the tree of knowledge' that distinguishes between good and evil.

The common features in all traditions were the connection between earth and heaven and between life in the here and now and the life of human ancestry. Spiritual qualities in different religions would nevertheless see a common link with the branches of the tree reaching up into the heavens and the roots of the tree going down deep into the earth to the subterranean waters from which the tree drew its life.

The poem draws upon the magnificent cedars and pine trees of Lebanon whose beauty could be compared to the Garden of Eden and its matchless beauty. Then in verse 11, we find the God of Creation handing power to the most ruthless of nations – Babylon. Nebuchadnezzar was to act on behalf of God. He overcame the might of the Assyrian empire and the great power of Egypt, all in one great battle at Carchemish in 605 BC.

The fall of Assyria and Egypt was a huge shock to all the other nations, none of whom were destined to reach such heights and all were destined for death in the realm below among mortal men (31:14). The fall of Assyria was to act as a warning to Egypt who had risen from the trauma of Carchemish, but judgement will fall upon Egypt and all those who look to her for protection. *"Yet you too, will be brought down with the trees of Eden to the earth below"* (31:18).

It is not easy to see the relevance of the metaphor of 'the tree of life' used here to convey a message to Egypt. The key lies in verse 10 which begins with the word *'Therefore'* and states as a word from God *"because it was* **proud** *of its height . . . I cast it aside."* It is significant that Ezekiel is seeing the God of Israel as the 'God of Creation' who holds the nations in his hands and controls their destiny. This is a theological concept that is developed later in the exile by Isaiah where we read such statements as *"Surely the nations are like a drop in a bucket; they are regarded as dust on the scales"* (Is 40:15).

Ezekiel is clearly searching for an understanding of why God would allow disaster to fall upon Jerusalem and the land of Judah and why he allows the Babylonians to prosper. God is working out his purposes of bringing justice into the nations and all empires that reach the heights bring judgement upon themselves and will fall along with all the foreign nations and 'uncircumcised' who will be brought down to Sheol.

Ezekiel does not specifically say at this point that God will eventually bring justice upon Babylon, because he is so full of indignation against Egypt. Jeremiah had reached an understanding of God's purposes earlier than this and he had already prophesied the fall of Babylon and sent it as a message of doom when Zedekiah went to meet Nebuchadnezzar in 593 as recorded in Jeremiah 51:59-64.

25 A LAMENT OVER PHARAOH Ezekiel 32: 1-16

In the twelfth year, in the twelfth month on the first day, the word of the Lord came to me: "Son of man, take up a lament concerning Pharaoh king of Egypt and say to him: You are like a lion among the nations; you are like a monster in the seas . . ."

Chapter 32 begins with a date, March 586 which shows us that everything in this chapter is coloured by events in Jerusalem that year, which is the year that the siege ended with the Babylonians breaking through the walls of Jerusalem, slaughtering the population and destroying the city. It consists of six small oracles and a lengthy lament featuring the underworld. The first short oracle is in verse 2 where Pharaoh king of Egypt is likened to a monster or dragon churning up the waters and creating chaos. The word for 'monster' is the same as that used in 29:3 where it referred to a crocodile in the Nile whereas this use of the word refers to the mythical monster of the seas. It was Pharaoh who had incited Zedekiah to revolt against the Babylonians and then failed to send his army to protect Jerusalem, so he is the monster who is blamed for the chaos that was taking place that year.

The second oracle is in 3-8 where the divine net refers to the Babylonians catching Zedekiah and drenching the land with blood. The third oracle in verses 9-10 foresees the fall of Egypt which will be seen by all the nations of the world. Verses 11-14 introduce Nebuchadnezzar as the instrument of Yahweh's judgement on Egypt. He will shatter the pride of Egypt, leaving her desolate and stripped of her wealth. The Babylonians certainly did invade Egypt, although there are no records showing that the land was left desolate. Verse 16 is a dirge mourning the fate of Egypt.

Verses 17 to the end of the chapter are also dated 586, the year of the destruction of Jerusalem, and Ezekiel uses it for a wailing or mourning song for Egypt whom, as we have seen, Ezekiel held primarily responsible for the disaster that befell Judah. The main interest for biblical scholars is the insight this gives us into Ezekiel's understanding of Sheol and the teaching that would have been prevalent among Israelites at that time. The three nations said to be resident in Sheol are Assyria, Elam and Meshech and Tubal (Ezek 32:22-37). These are said to be numbered among the uncircumcised and those slain by the sword and had been given dishonourable deaths – dispatched to Sheol. They are mixed in with some of the men who were regarded as heroes by their fellow countrymen who were given honourable funerals described in verse 27, with their swords placed under their heads. But they were all sent down into the underworld among the uncircumcised who had terrorised Israel, the land of the living and were now banished by God. Egypt would be among these groups in Sheol, because of the terror she had brought to the land of Israel.

Ezekiel's antipathy towards Egypt was shared by Jeremiah who strongly warned the survivors of the destruction of Jerusalem not to go to Egypt but to stay in the land and make peace with the Babylonians. *"If you stay in this land, I will build you up and not tear you down; I will plant you and not uproot you"* (Jer 42:10). Jeremiah also said as a word from the Lord, *"All those who are determined to go to Egypt to settle there will die by the sword, famine and plague"* (Jer 42:17).

All the warnings from both Jeremiah and Ezekiel did not succeed in preventing the people of Judah from putting their trust in Egypt as they had done for many years. In 312 the pro-Egypt party was still influential in Jerusalem. Under the leadership of Ptolemy, Egypt attacked Gaza, driving out the Greeks and they went on to attack Jerusalem, the record of which was preserved by Agatharchides:

"There are a people called Jews, and they dwell in a city which is the strongest of all cities, and which the inhabitants call Jerusalem. They are accustomed to rest on every seventh day; at these times they do not take up arms . . . But they lift up their hands in their holy places and pray until the evening. When Ptolemy the son of Lagi entered into this city with his army, these people, in observing their foolish custom, instead of guarding their city, suffered their country to submit to a cruel master; and their law was thus clearly proven to command a foolish practice." [4]

He then carried more than 100,000 into slavery in Egypt. The warnings of both Jeremiah and Ezekiel had been ignored at their peril.

---

4 Quoted by Josephus, *Contra Ap* i, 209-210.

26 LIFE AFTER DEATH IN SHEOL Ezekiel 32:17–32

In the twelfth year, on the fifteenth day of the month, the word of the Lord came to me: "Son of man, wail for the hordes of Egypt and consign to the earth below both her and the daughters of the mighty nations, with those who go down to the pit . . ."

The lament for Pharaoh that we studied in the previous passage concludes with a chant that consigns Egypt to being made desolate by the Babylonians. The rest of chapter 32 which we are studying today begins with wailing for the hordes of Egypt who will be consigned to the earth below along with many other mighty nations.

This is of huge significance in providing for us the understanding of Sheol that was current in Ezekiel's lifetime. It also puts into historical perspective the rise and fall of great empires, ending as it begins by Pharaoh and all the hordes of Egypt who spread terror in the land of the living, being consigned to be numbered among the uncircumcised in Sheol.

Sheol is a realm below the ground where all the dishonourable dead are held captive, they are confined to the pit. It is a place of disgrace where those who exercised great or small power in the land of the living will be held in punishment for their actions. There is no distinction between those whom the nations honoured and others. Those who were mighty leaders of nations during their life on earth will also be laid among the uncircumcised and those slain by the sword.

Thus Sheol becomes a place of life after death where justice is exercised upon those who spread terror in the land of the living. Their graves are in the depths of the pit. This is where all those who spread terror during their lives bear their shame down in the pit. Those warriors who were greatly honoured by the nations by being buried with their swords placed underneath their heads would be particularly punished as they lie among all the uncircumcised who went down to the grave with their weapons of war – there will be no distinctions among them down in the pit.

In this vision of Sheol Ezekiel sees people of all ranks being consigned to punishment in the life hereafter for their sins, particularly for the violence they exercised and the terror they spread among the nations.

It is of particular interest to see Ezekiel's view of the rise and fall of empires in the context of the sovereignty of God. It is God who consigns to the earth below the powerful empires of the nations. He sees the leaders of the mighty Empire of Egypt together with all her satellites and those who put their trust in Egypt – all sent down into the earth below. The Empire of Assyria is there with the whole of her army that once ruled a large area of the earth. Their graves are down in the pit alongside others who died violent deaths through the sword. Elam is there, bearing their shame alongside the uncircumcised who spread terror among the nations in the land of the living. Meshech and Tubal are there in their graves lying with the uncircumcised warriors whom they killed, suffering their punishment alongside others who stalked the land of the living. Pharaoh was there in the company of the uncircumcised. So too were the kings of Edom and all their rulers, together with the rulers of Sidon and other nations that were consigned to the pit in disgrace.

We have already noted that Ezekiel's presentation was within the context of the sovereignty of God. He saw the hand of God guiding the nations and even using empires such as Babylon that he described as *"the most ruthless of nations"* for working out his purposes. In this policy, Ezekiel was following the teaching of Jeremiah who had declared as a word from God to the kings of Edom, Moab, Ammon, Tyre and Sidon, *"Now I will hand all your countries over to my servant Nebuchadnezzar king of Babylon"* (Jer 27:6). Jeremiah had followed that statement in the next verse with the declaration that Babylon would exercise power *"until the time for his land comes"* implying that judgement would come upon him and his Empire when some other great kings would arise and subjugate him.

If Ezekiel had lived in the lifetime of many alive today, he would have seen the fall of the British Empire, the Ottoman Empire, Germany's Third Reich, the Empire of Japan, the fall of the USSR, the rise of America and China, and economic power draining from nations into global corporations whose only loyalty is to shareholders. He would have seen the Jews back in the land of Israel as a nuclear power exercising military might in the same way as the Gentile nations.

27 THE ROLE OF THE WATCHMAN Ezekiel 33:1-6

The word of the Lord came to me: "Son of man, speak to your countrymen and say to them: 'When I bring the sword against the land, and the people of the land choose one of their men and make him their watchman, and he sees the sword coming against the land and blows the trumpet to warn the people, then if anyone hears the trumpet but does not take warning and the sword comes and takes his life, his blood will be on his own head' . . ."

Chapter 33 represents the beginning of the third major section in the book of Ezekiel. It resumes the account of the ministry of the prophet which covered chapters 1 – 24 with its warnings about what would happen to Jerusalem unless there were repentance and turning away from idolatry in the city. Chapter 33 begins a new phase in the ministry of Ezekiel. It is clearly dated to the year 586 and the fall of Jerusalem and marks the beginning of Ezekiel's teaching taking on a new significance when there was no longer morning and evening sacrifice taking place in the temple in Jerusalem. Ezekiel had the responsibility of teaching the exiles in Babylon a new understanding of God and new ways of worshipping him.

This chapter begins the new phase of teaching that follows on from chapter 24. The sequence had been interrupted by the inclusion of eight chapters of oracles against foreign nations including a concentration upon the responsibility of Egypt in the fate of Jerusalem and the land of Judah. Chapter 33 begins with teaching on the role of the watchman which is a development of the theme outlined in chapter 18 by presenting teaching to the exiles on individual responsibility for sin which was a new concept in Israel. Ezekiel's purpose at that point had been to counteract the belief among the exiles that they were paying the price for the sins of their fathers. Ezekiel had to teach them that they too were sinners and that the judgement that was falling upon those left in the city of Jerusalem did not mean that they were the most wicked. The whole nation of Judah had been involved to some extent in idolatry – either up in the mountain sanctuaries on the high places, or in the streets of Jerusalem where altars had been set up and whole families were indulging in idolatry as detailed in Jeremiah 7:16-19 and 30-34.

Traditionally the role of the watchman had been to keep watch during the hours of the night so that the citizens could sleep peacefully in their beds without fear of sudden attack. The task of the watchman was to recognise danger and be ready at all times to blow the trumpet of warning so that the defences of the city could be rapidly mobilised to counteract the danger. If the watchman fell asleep, or in some other way failed to blow the trumpet of warning, and a city suffered an attack and lives were lost, the watchman would be held responsible for their blood. If, on the other hand the watchman had blown the trumpet and the people had ignored the warning, their blood would have been on their own heads.

Watchmen were also appointed for the army when they set up camp and there would be a number of watches during the night so that each man on duty would only have a few hours before he was relieved by another watchman. We read this in the story of Gideon where he mounted his attack at the beginning of the middle watch when the eyes of the new guard had not yet adjusted to the darkness (Judg 7:19).

Shepherds also used to bring all their sheep together and keep them in a joint sheepfold overnight when the shepherds would take it in turn to act as watchmen, their task was to watch out for wild beasts who might attack the flock, or thieves who might come to steal a lamb. Jesus used this as an illustration of his own role as the Good Shepherd who would lay down his life for the sheep (John 10:11).

A modern example of the role of the watchman occurred in the early 1980s when video recorders were just becoming popular with violent films, many of which were being seen by children. During the Parliamentary Video Enquiry 1983/84, Christians throughout the country were asked to act as watchmen for their town, to protect the local community. They were given a list of video films classified by the Director of Public Prosecutions as obscene so they could visit local shops and identify harmful films and report them to the police. Thousands of Christians acted as 'watchmen' to protect their communities.

28 EZEKIEL AS A WATCHMAN Ezekiel 33:7-11

"Son of man, I have made you a watchman for the house of Israel, so hear the word I speak and give them warning from me. When I say to the wicked, 'O wicked man, you will surely die,' and you do not speak out to dissuade him from his ways, that wicked man will die for his sin, and I will hold you accountable for his blood . . ."

This passage marks a confirmation given to Ezekiel of his calling as a prophet among the exiled people of Israel. The first three chapters of the book of Ezekiel describe his original calling, just five years into the exile. The words now being recorded mark a significant milestone in the history of Judah and of the exiles in Babylon with the news that Jerusalem had fallen, and that the temple had been destroyed. The loss of the temple priesthood put Ezekiel in a position of chief priest among the exiles. His original calling was to be a spokesman for God, *"You must speak my words to them, whether they listen or fail to listen"* (Ezek 2:7). Now the emphasis is upon a more rounded ministry that included elements of watchman, pastor, teacher, prophet, and even evangelist.

Traditionally in Israel the watchman not only had responsibility for recognising danger and blowing the trumpet of warning, but one of his duties was to blow the trumpet announcing the beginning of a feast, such as a new moon or a full moon. Ezekiel is now told that his watchman role among the exiles was not only to recognise when God was warning people of sinful behaviour, but his responsibility was to persuade the people to change their behaviour. If he did not do this, he would be responsible for the people dying in their sins. This should be a salutary warning to all those who are in pastoral charge of churches today or who are called to preach the gospel. It is not sufficient simply to blow a trumpet of warning, the task of the pastor/ preacher/teacher is to change the behaviour of sinful people.

Ezekiel was given an example because the destruction of Jerusalem had come as a tremendous shock to the exiles, and they were recognising their part in the responsibility for God having allowed this to happen which was due to their own sinful behaviour. Many of them must have either been involved in idolatry or they certainly knew what was going on among their friends and neighbours, before the exile. They were not only feeling guilty, but they were feeling helpless – some of them were feeling suicidal, *"How then can we live?"* This is where Ezekiel's role as theological teacher as well as pastor became essential. He had to assure the people that God took no pleasure in the death of the wicked, but he was always more ready to forgive than people were to repent and turn to him for forgiveness and restoration. This was where the teacher role bordered on the work of the evangelist – "*Turn! Turn from your evil ways!" (33.11).*

It was at this point In the history of the exile in Babylon that Ezekiel took on a new role for which all his previous experience, including his ecstatic visions, had prepared him. It was his responsibility to carry out a task of great creativity – actually creating a new community of faith, with clear teaching about the nature and purposes of God for his chosen people – for giving them vision and purpose based upon an understanding of their own history and spiritual heritage.

It was Ezekiel, more than any other person, who was responsible for protecting the people from the powerful influence of idolatry in Babylon and for establishing such major institutions as the Sabbath and its central role in the spiritual life of the nation, and the Synagogue, not only as the central meeting place for the community and community activities, but as a place of worship where both collectively and individually the presence of God could be experienced.

Ezekiel's first task in this new post-Jerusalem era was to teach the people a basic understanding of the nature of God – of his love and justice that together showed his desire for a new and living relationship with his people, turning them away from ways of death into ways of joyous, victorious living. This would later be the characteristic that Ezekiel was to teach about having a new heart, and living within a new covenant relationship with God that would transform everything around them and they would live in his presence and experience his loving prosperity. Ezekiel was already receiving the revelation of this new relationship with God of which he was the herald – *"I will give you a new heart and put a new spirit in you"* (Ezek 36:26).

29 INDIVIDUAL RESPONSIBILITY FOR SIN
Ezekiel 33:12-20

"Therefore, Son of man, say to your countrymen, 'The righteousness of the righteous man will not save him when he disobeys, and the wickedness of the wicked man will not cause him to fall when he turns from it. The righteous man, if he sins, will not be allowed to live because of his former righteousness . . .' Yet your countrymen say, 'The way of the Lord is not just.' But it is their way that is not just. If a righteous man turns from his righteousness and does evil, he will die for it . . ."

This piece is an expansion of Ezekiel 18 which introduced a new understanding of the justice of God, leading them away from corporate responsibility for wrongdoing to the recognition of some form of individual responsibility. In chapter 18, the principle was established that dismissed the old proverb, *"The fathers eat sour grapes, and the children's teeth are set on edge" (Jer 31:29).* This was being used to account for the exile and to excuse the exiles from any responsibility for what had happened to Jerusalem. The principle of individual responsibility was established to the extent that each of them had to accept some accountability for what had happened in the nation.

The statement repeated here, that God did not take any pleasure in the death of the wicked, was a central feature of the teaching set out in chapter 18. If the wicked man repented, he would live, but if a righteous man did wicked things, his former righteousness would not save him. The climax of the chapter was a declaration by God that he would judge each one by their ways. Therefore, repentance was the major requirement for all, and turning away from their offensive actions whereby God would offer them a new heart and a new spirit, was a foreshadowing of the major message that Ezekiel was now delivering.

The difference between the teaching in chapter 18 and here in chapter 33 is the fact that in chapter 18 Jerusalem had still been standing and the temple was still observing morning and evening sacrifices for sins. This had ensured that the nation was always in a right relationship with God through the principle of corporate responsibility. Ezekiel now had to counteract this. The first sign of this new teaching was given in Psalm 79.8 which comes from this period, *"Do not hold against us the sins of the fathers. May your mercy come quickly to meet us, for we are in desperate need"*.

Ezekiel's teaching on repentance and individual responsibility for sin was highly influenced by his compatriot Jeremiah, and the 8th century prophets, such as Isaiah of Jerusalem who hated the whole practice of animal sacrifices: *"The multitude of your sacrifices – what are they to me? Says the Lord. I have had more than enough of burnt offerings, of rams and the fat of fattened animals; I have no pleasure in the blood of bulls and lambs and goats"* (Is 1:11). Jeremiah's message on forgiveness of sins came following his visit to the potter's shop where he was given a message relating to all nations at all times (Jer 18:1-10).

One of the major results of the destruction of Jerusalem and the loss of the temple and the cessation of priestly sacrifices, was that the people of Israel in Babylon began to realise that they needed to take responsibility for their own actions with regard to sin and repentance, and not to rely upon a temple-based sacrificial system offering vicarious absolution.

This was a major turning point in the spiritual life of the nation. It gave Ezekiel the opportunity for introducing to Israel a new conception of the justice of God which had for generations been based upon the basic principle of 'eye for eye, tooth for tooth', and this was embedded in the principal of corporate responsibility. Ezekiel was teaching an entirely new concept based upon individual relationships with God such as they had never previously conceived. The relationship with God was always on a corporate basis and God only spoke to them through Moses or appointed prophets. The new teaching showed that God could have a personal relationship with each one, and that each one could hear from him and speak to him through prayer.

This was an entirely new concept and paved the way both for the establishment of the practices linked with observing the Sabbath and laid the foundation of the Synagogue as a place of prayer, teaching, and worship. The justice of God that was being challenged by the exiles was now being seen in a new light and a new relationship with God which not only made each one responsible for their own individual behaviour, but it opened up each one to the blessings from God in their individual lives.

30 JERUSALEM'S DESTRUCTION EXPLAINED
Ezekiel 33:21-29

In the twelfth year of our exile, in the tenth month on the fifth day, a man who had escaped from Jerusalem came to me and said, "The city has fallen!" Now the evening before the man arrived, the hand of the Lord was upon me, and he opened my mouth before the man came to me in the morning.

The date given at the beginning of this reading presents some difficulties because Jeremiah has given us a specific date for the fall of the city of Jerusalem, and the date given by Ezekiel would be 17 months later which is clearly an extraordinary long time for news to reach Babylon. In Judah they would have been using the Hebraic calendar where the New Year is in the autumn, whereas the Babylonian calendar has the New Year in the spring which would reduce the gap but still leave it with far too long a gap for the news to be transmitted.

We know that there was regular communication between the two cities so we can only conclude that we don't know the date when this refugee from the destruction of Jerusalem arrived with his eyewitness testimony. Ezekiel had been expecting this news since the day he heard that the siege of Jerusalem had begun which was in the year 588 and is recorded in 24:1. In the same chapter Ezekiel was given forewarning of the day when he would receive news of the fall of Jerusalem. *"At that time your mouth will be opened; you will speak with him and will no longer be silent"* (24: 27). He had already begun teaching a post-temple message as we have seen.

Ezekiel says that the Lord opened his mouth before the man arrived in the morning. He says, *"I was no longer silent."* Once again, this is difficult for us to explain because there is no record of Ezekiel having been struck dumb beforehand, although at the time of his call to ministry he was warned that there would be occasions when he would be made silent and unable to speak to the people (3:26). The best explanation for this is that all the prophets sometimes use the phrase about God opening their mouth to refer to receiving a word from God.

Ezekiel is concerned about the news he had received of the survivors in the land of Judah raising questions about ownership of the land. Ezekiel's answer is that the disaster is not yet complete, but that those left among the ruins will also fall by the sword, and those out in the countryside would not escape. The whole land of Judah is destined to become a desolate waste. The reason given for this devastation had already been given by Ezekiel in many warnings from God.

Verses 25 and 26 are central to the message of Ezekiel, showing the justice of God. They summarise the charges against the people of Judah who had been deliberately disobeying the commandments of God in regard to dietary rules, worshipping idols, shedding innocent blood and immorality. These were all warnings given by Jeremiah in his Temple Sermon (Jer 7:1-12). *"You rely on your sword"* most likely means that they used violence in their disputes with neighbours since it occurs here in the context of domestic disputes, rather than military conflict.

All this evidence of lawless behaviour and defiance of the word of God, or the warnings sent to them through the prophets, forms the reason why God had removed his presence from Jerusalem and his cover from over the land so that disaster had come upon the people. In offering this reason for what had happened to Jerusalem there is no mention here of action by the Babylonians. Everything that had happened was due to the hand of God. It was pointless for those remaining in the land to have disputes over ownership. God's answer to all their questions was, *"Should you then possess the land?"* God was fully justified in removing his protection and this was a demonstration of his justice.

Israel had been warned by God at Mount Sinai that there were conditions as part of the covenant. If they broke the Law, especially in regard to the worship of other gods, God's covenant promises would be invalid. This was why he had allowed the enemy to carry out such destruction. *"Then they will know that I am the Lord, when I have made the land a desolate waste because of all the detestable things they have done"* (33:29). This was part of the justice of God that Israel had yet to learn. It was probably the hardest lesson, whuch had still not been understood by the time of Jesus who often used his parables such as the 'prodigal son' to try to teach them about the justice of God.

31 EZEKIEL IN HIS HOME GROUP Ezekiel 33:30-33

"As for you, Son of man, your countrymen are talking together about you by the walls and at the doors of the houses, saying to each other, 'Come and hear the message that has come from the Lord.' My people come to you, as they usually do, and sit before you to listen to your words, but they do not put them into practice. With their mouths they express devotion, but their hearts are greedy for unjust gain. Indeed, to them you are nothing more than one who sings love songs with a beautiful voice and plays an instrument well."

This is a fascinating little insight into life among the exiles from Judah who were living in settlements scattered around Babylonia. There is no date given to this description of an incident in the home of Ezekiel at Tel Abib. It sounds much more likely to have occurred earlier in the exile rather than in its present setting, just after news had reached Babylon of the destruction of Jerusalem. The reference to some of Ezekiel's group being *"greedy for unjust gain"* indicates that they had been in Babylon long enough to be involved in the local economy where we know that many of them became rich merchants.

We know that little groups of elders used to come regularly to sit at Ezekiel's feet to hear any word he had recently received from the Lord, and to listen to his teaching. This enabled the elders to go back to teach what they had received. In this way the whole community in exile would receive teaching that would keep their heritage alive and enable people to memorise portions of the Torah which they could teach to their children.

The meeting that is described here, however, is not a gathering of the elders, it is a coming together of people in his own local community at Tel Abib for what could be genuinely described as a house meeting – the first record of such a meeting before we reach the Early Church in the New Testament. Ezekiel is reminded that he is becoming quite well known in the local community and his house meetings were growing in popularity. People all over the town were talking about him and his regular group were urging other people among their friends and neighbours to come to hear this amazing man who was growing in popularity. He was not only a good speaker but he was also a musician with a lovely voice. No doubt Ezekiel had learned to sing the Psalms when he was an active priest in the temple in Jerusalem. Now he was doing this on a regular basis in his 'house church' community.

The personal word he received from God would certainly have been a damper if he was beginning to feel pleased with his growing popularity. The word was, *"They listen to your words, but they do not put them into practice."* That is the sort of bad news that no preacher wants to hear. No preacher wants to be known as 'popular' – or that no one takes his words seriously. In fact, some of the people listening to Ezekiel were not only ignoring his teaching but they were *"greedy for unjust gain"*.

Another reason for believing that this little incident occurred earlier in the exile, is that from all the information we have available about the growth and development of the exile population, house fellowships were the earliest form of community meetings before the formation of knessets, that later developed into Synagogues. The practice of lighting candles on Friday evenings began very early in the exile where families observed the Sabbath meal and had times of prayer for family members, for those left behind in Jerusalem and of course praying for the City and the temple.

One or two families then began to meet together and, from these informal gatherings, house meetings began on Shabbat creating the demand for meeting places, which paved the way for the formation of the Synagogue in each of the settlements which became very precious. In fact, they were so loved that when the exiles returned to the land and rebuilt the temple, they also built synagogues in each of their local communities which was a lasting legacy of the exile.

The synagogues played a large part in the life of every village or town and were of far greater local significance than the temple. Jesus spoke in local synagogues and Paul made a practice everywhere he went of first visiting the local synagogue. House meetings came into the life of communities of Christians through the ministry of the Apostles from the earliest days after Pentecost. This was a lasting memorial to the communities of the exile such as was first seen in Ezekiel's home.

32 REVIEW AND OVERVIEW OF EZEKIEL 34 – 37

We have reached a major turning point in the overall story being presented by the Prophet Ezekiel. That story began five years into the exile in Babylon with a violent storm that led to a profound spiritual experience in Ezekiel's life, through which God called him into a special ministry among the exiles. His calling was to a people who saw themselves as unjustly deserted by their God and victims of a cruel dictatorship. Despite the false prophecies of some among them of an early return there were no signs of those hopes becoming true. Some of the exiles among them were already beginning to adjust to life among the Babylonians (Ezek 20:32).

Ezekiel had the task of convincing them that the God of Israel had by no means deserted them. He was, in fact, the God of all the world who held the nations in his hands and all that had happened was within his will. Ezekiel had to teach the people, through the story running through the book, that they were part of a sinful generation and God was treating them as their sins deserved.

This reached a climax in chapters 20 – 23 with the allegory of the two sisters depicting the judgement of Israel and Judah that had resulted in the exile. Ezekiel had yet to teach the people that they were in Babylon to become a transformed people, to return and rebuild Jerusalem and the towns of Judah.

In chapter 24, written in 588, Ezekiel noted the day Nebuchadnezzar began his siege of Jerusalem. It coincided with the death of Ezekiel's wife and the statement that God would not spare the temple from destruction. There were still many exiles who believed that Jerusalem was inviolable – that God would protect both the city and the temple from foreign invasion. Ezekiel had to tell them that this was utterly false. He had seen in a vision, which he had described to their elders, coals taken from the altar and divine fire scattered across the city, symbolising that it was God himself who was bringing judgement upon the city and that God himself was about to desecrate his sanctuary (24:21).

Chapters 25 – 32 have prophecies against the nations who were Israel's neighbours, all of whom had done offensive things. None of them had come to the aid of Judah in her hour of need and many of them had openly rejoiced at her downfall. God was assuring the exiles that in the same way as he was exercising judgement upon his own people for their sinfulness, he would bring judgement upon those who rejoiced at the mishap of the people of Israel.

This is the point we have now reached at the end of chapter 33 where a man who had escaped, reported that Jerusalem had fallen. Ezekiel had already been forewarned that '*the delight of your eyes*' (his wife and the temple) would be taken from him. For him the news of the destruction of Jerusalem brought both distress and relief. His prophecy had been fiercely rejected by many people. It had now been fulfilled. He was a true prophet. God had indeed spoken through him.

We come now to the central point in the Book of Ezekiel with chapters 34 – 37 which are full of good news. It begins with judgement upon the whole leadership of the people of Israel including the monarchy. This all had to go, so that God could do a new work of restoration. God himself will be a shepherd to his people, caring for the weak and finding the strays. He will gather them from all the places where they had been scattered.

Chapter 35 gives assurance of God cleansing the land that had been annexed by the people of Edom who had defiled it with their gods. Yahweh the God of Israel was going to deal with them and reclaim his land, so Ezekiel was instructed to proclaim the good news to the mountains of Israel. It would not only be the land that is cleansed but God was going to wash the people clean from their sins and give them a new heart and pour out his Holy Spirit upon them (36:24-27).

Chapter 37 has the wonderful message of national resurrection. The dry bones become filled with new life as the whole nation is raised from the dead and God brings his people up from the grave. They will not only be new people, but God will give them a king of the line of David who will be a Good Shepherd to them and God himself will establish a covenant of peace with them. He will plant his sanctuary among them and abide with his people for ever.

Now we will resume our study of the text.

33 THE SHEPHERDS OF ISRAEL Ezekiel 34:1-10

The word of the Lord came to me: "Son of man, prophesy against the shepherds of Israel; prophesy and say to them: 'This is what the Sovereign Lord says: Woe to the shepherds of Israel who only take care of themselves! Should not shepherds take care of the flock? You eat the curds, clothe yourselves with the wool and slaughter the choice animals, but you do not take care of the flock. You have not strengthened the weak or healed the sick or bound up the injured' . . ."

This chapter is a somewhat strange intrusion into the contemporary ministry of Ezekiel among the exiles in Babylon. It is as if he has taken time out after the shock news of the destruction of Jerusalem and the temple and the widespread destruction across the land of Judah. He had been prophesying this as something that would inevitably happen unless there were repentance and turning to the Lord, but the reality still came as a brutal shock to him.

In this chapter Ezekiel looks back over the history of Israel tracing events that led up to the situation today where large numbers of the people of Israel were scattered across the nations, many of whom would never return to the land, but would be lost for ever. Ezekiel would have been spreading the situation he faced before the Lord in prayer and seeking answers to his questions as to why God would allow such a tragedy to come upon his people. The result of his thinking is gathered in this chapter.

Chapter 34 is in four sections that have been edited together. They each occupy about a quarter of the chapter. The first section is in verses 1-10 and the second section is in verses 11-16. The third is in 17-24 and the fourth is in 25-31.

Ezekiel 34:1-10 begins with a powerful charge against the rulers of the nation. Ezekiel follows Jeremiah in using the term 'shepherds' for the rulers of the nation. They both use this as a very general term encompassing all those who hold power in the nation. They would have been the group of advisers around the monarch who were responsible for exercising political policy, but it would no doubt also include people with economic power over industry and commerce and the top religious authorities who were also influential in the affairs of the nation. Ezekiel was addressing them both.

In Jeremiah's ministry, he singled out these religious leaders for special treatment; naming them as 'prophets and priests', whom he regularly accused of leading the people astray both by false teaching and by their personal lifestyles. Jeremiah specifically charged the scribes with distorting the word of God in order to give authority to their own false teaching. He said that *"the lying pen of the scribes"* had falsely handled the Torah (Jer 8:8) and that *"the prophets prophesy lies, the priests rule by their own authority, and my people love it this way"* (Jer 5:31).

Ezekiel accuses the shepherds of not caring for the weak and the sick or those who were injured. Those who exercised power in the nation should have a special care for those with special needs. The rulers had not exercised proper pastoral care as shepherds of the flock. They had ruled 'harshly and brutally', taking care of their own interests, and neglecting the interests of others and also of the welfare of the whole community.

The shepherd was the ideal metaphor for those who held power over other people's lives in the same way as the shepherd cared for his sheep who were totally dependent upon him for their protection and for leading them to the right places for food and water. King David was the ideal king and he started life as a simple shepherd, but he had practical experience of protecting his sheep from wild animals and caring for them as the rulers of the nation should care for the people.

The charges against the rulers of the nation were followed by the declaration, *"This is what the Sovereign Lord says: I am against the shepherds and will hold them accountable for my flock. I will remove them from tending the flock."* (v. 10). Accountability is the major theme of this passage. It establishes the fact that leadership is not for the furtherance of self-interest but for the good of the whole community or nation.

The people of Israel had been led by self-centred foolish men who had misused their power for their own advantage, and they were responsible for the disaster that had come upon the nation – God was holding them accountable for his people. There could be no more fearful declaration than this, and it is a pronouncement that applies to everyone who has any sort of responsibilities for the lives of other people.

34 CARING FOR THE FLOCK Ezekiel 34:11-16

"For this is what the Sovereign Lord says: I myself will search for my sheep and look after them. As a shepherd looks after his scattered flock when he is with them, so will I look after my sheep. I will rescue them from all the places where they were scattered on a day of clouds and darkness . . ."

There is a sharp change of tone from verse 11 emphasising the harsh condemnation of the rulers of Israel whom God was holding responsible for the scattering of the people that had followed the destruction of the towns and countryside of Judah, as well as Jerusalem. The focus here turned from what foolish and selfish men had done in their misuse of power, to what God was going to do. His action in shepherding the sheep would present a model. He would reverse the situation that had been created by these false shepherds and bring his people back to the land of Israel that he had given to their forefathers. *"I myself will tend my sheep"* is the theme developed here.

The picture of God himself visiting the nations where the exiles were living in scattered communities, such as they were around Babylon where Ezekiel was ministering, must have been a beautiful picture for the exiles to hear. Ezekiel said this to the elders so that they could go back to their communities and bring this as a word from the Lord – a promise of his tender presence among them and his care for them.

We know that a considerable number of the exiles were engaged in agricultural pursuits and some of them would have been shepherds. This picture of God himself searching for the lost and taking them to good pastures would have reminded them of David's words in Psalm 23, *"The Lord is my Shepherd"*. This picture would have been readily accepted and would enable them to have fresh understanding of God. The picture Ezekiel was presenting went even farther in communicating a message to the exiles – not only to those working in agriculture, but to every one of them whatever their occupation. The promise was that God himself would search for each one of them and that the day would come when *"they will feed in a rich pasture on the mountains of Israel" (v. 14)*.

Jeremiah had said that God would bring them back to the land, but this is the first promise in Ezekiel's ministry that the exile would come to an end and the people of Israel would be taken back to their own land where they would once again enjoy the mountains of Israel and its rich pastures. This was a promise that was not just a hope that the people had had ever since they first arrived and hung their harps on the poplars beside the canals of Babylon where they wept and longed to see Jerusalem (Ps 137).

It was not just a hope. It was an actual promise from God. It meant that he had not forgotten them despite all the terrible news that they had been hearing of what was happening to the city they loved and the people to whom many were related. The God of their fathers about whose wonderful deeds they had so often heard was not just the God of the past, but he was active today and he was promising to search for his people and bring them back into the promised land. His word was, *"I will search for the lost and bring back the strays. I will bind up the injured and strengthen the weak"* (v. 16).

This picture of the shepherd caring for his sheep is clearly reflected in the teaching of Jesus who would, of course, have been familiar with the teaching of Ezekiel. The parable Jesus told of the shepherd searching for a lost sheep in Luke 15 echoes the words of Ezekiel. Jesus used the story of the shepherd's joy at finding a lost sheep to teach people about the nature of God and his care for each one of his people. In John's gospel this teaching was made even more personal to Jesus' own personal care for his disciples, *"I am the good Shepherd; I know my sheep and my sheep know me"* (John 10:14).

The final word in this piece is of great significance. It says, *"I will shepherd the flock with justice."* The whole concept of the justice of God was slowly being developed by the prophets of Israel since the time of Amos in the 8th century who called for *"justice to roll on like a river"* in Israel (Amos 5:24), and Isaiah, who believed God would be exalted by his justice when he humbled mankind (Is 5:16). Ezekiel sees the justice of God in caring for his sheep and fulfilling his promises to his people.

35 THE LORD JUDGES HIS SHEEP Ezekiel 34:17-24

As for you, my flock, this is what the Sovereign Lord says: "I will judge between one sheep and another, and between rams and goats. Is it not enough for you to feed on the good pasture? Must you also trample the rest of your pasture with your feet? Is it not enough for you to drink clear water? Must you also muddy the rest with your feet? Must my flock feed on what you have trampled and drink what you have muddied with your feet? . . ."

This passage introduces a new theme. It is no longer the relationship between shepherd and sheep that is the focal point – but the relationships between the sheep themselves. The concept of the justice of God had just been mentioned at the end of the previous passage, now it becomes centre stage. He will judge between sheep and sheep and the measure of justice will be in the individual relationships between each of the sheep – how they care for each other. The example is given of the strong sheep feasting when they reach the good pasture first and eating their fill, without any thought for the rest of the flock who were coming behind. They thoughtlessly trampled the good pasture underfoot, thus denying it to the weaker sheep.

The strong sheep did the same when they reached the edge of the water. They just plunged into it slaking their thirst and when they had drunk all they wanted they churned up the mud so that the water was polluted for the others to drink. It was this thoughtlessness and lack of care for other people that was the measure upon which judgement was going to be meted out to each one.

The word of God was that he himself would judge between the sheep and they would be judged on the basis of their treatment of other sheep. This passage in Ezekiel must have been well known to Jesus because it is clearly linked to the New Testament story told by Jesus of the end-time judgement between sheep and goats (Matt 25:31-33).

In the Ezekiel story God would *"judge between one sheep and another, and between rams and goats."* In the story Jesus told, the separation was between sheep and goats – the sheep were blessed, and the goats were not. Ezekiel makes the distinction between fat sheep and lean sheep, and the basic criteria upon which judgement is to be passed in both stories is on the practical behaviour of individuals.

The fat sheep in Ezekiel's story are those who use their weight to drive the weaker sheep away from the feeding place. In the story Matthew reports, judgement is given on the basis of whether or not each individual had given practical assistance and support to others who were in need. The needy were in fact the Lord himself, although he was unknown to those who gave him assistance.

Ezekiel's story introduced an entirely unexpected element – bringing in David, the ideal King of Israel. He will be the new servant of God who will act as Shepherd of the sheep and tend to all their needs. He has been brought in here as a kind of Messianic figure who would be the servant of God caring for the needs of his people. He would be the ideal ruler of Israel gathering the flock and leading them in their restoration of Israel.

This entry of David as an ideal King is the earliest mention of a Messianic era in the future. In its setting here, following the tragedy of the destruction of Israel and the scattering of the people among the nations, it has a particular appeal to the exiles. There would come a day when the exile would end, and then the way would be open for them to return to the promised land and they would no longer have the crooked leadership that had led to disaster.

The God of Israel would personally intervene and establish a new era with an ideal leader who would come from the line of David, the servant of God. He would gather the strays, the lost sheep of Israel and Judah scattered among the countries of the Assyrians and Babylonians, and he would tend them carefully. He would also be a righteous judge who would ensure justice between each of the sheep so that relationships would be harmonious and fair to each one.

No longer would some people be plundered, exploited, or enslaved, but each one would look to their Messianic leader to establish this new kingdom of righteous relationships and the Lord himself would be their God. This ideal Messianic kingdom sets the scene for the final section in this chapter which foreshadows the coming of the Messianic Age.

36 THE MESSIANIC KINGDOM Ezekiel 34:25-31

I will make a covenant of peace with them and rid the land of wild beasts so that they may live in the desert and sleep in the forest in safety. I will bless them and the places surrounding my hill. I will send down showers in season; there will be showers of blessing.

Ezekiel sees God himself intervening in the life of the nation in these desperate days. The background to this, as we have been seeing in earlier parts of this chapter, is that Ezekiel hears God saying, *"I myself will search for my sheep and look after them"* (34:12).

Ezekiel was foreseeing the time when Assyria and Babylon would give up the scattered flock of Israel. The day would come when Babylon would be broken and the Lord would gather his scattered flock back into the land where, *"They will feed in a rich pasture on the mountains of Israel"* (34:14). In this last part of chapter 34 the themes introduced in each of the three earlier sections are brought together. They form what is the earliest appearance of the 'Messianic Hope of Israel' for the postexilic period. It is significant that Ezekiel is led to this message so soon after the devastating news had reached him of the destruction of Jerusalem and the temple. It marks a major change of direction in his thinking.

The theme now is in contrast to that of verses 11-16 where the shepherd is searching the wild countryside of ravines and settlements for the lost sheep of Israel. The theme of judgement is also dropped, and this passage builds upon the vision of David, the ideal servant of the Lord, becoming the leader of the people in the new postexilic age. The figures of the shepherd and the sheep now disappear and are replaced by the Edenic conditions of the Messianic Age.

This is clearly based upon the promises of a covenant of peace in Leviticus 26:4-6. The promise there, is of rain in the right season to yield crops on the ground and fruit on the trees. There will be great harvests with plenty of food to eat and all the people will live safely in the land. The promise is, *"I will grant peace in the land, and you will lie down and no one will make you afraid. I will remove savage beasts from the land, and the sword will not pass through your country"*

(Lev 26:6). This promise of peace and plenty is enriched by scenes originating from the Garden of Eden. The promise is that they will not only be secure in their own land and freed from the persecution of other nations, but the land will also be freed from savage wild animals so that they will be able to sleep soundly either out in the desert or in the forests.

This kind of tranquil countryside enjoying peaceful relationships with other nations had been described back in the reign of Hezekiah by the prophet Micah, *"Nation will not take up sword against nation, nor will they train for war any more"* (Micah 4:3). This was a word that had earlier come from Isaiah of Jerusalem in the 8th century who foresaw the day when many peoples would want to go up to Jerusalem to hear the word of the Lord, beating their swords into ploughshares and seeking for God to teach them his ways (Is 2:3-4).

Ezekiel was foreseeing the Messianic Age being a return to the original peace and tranquillity of the Garden of Eden before the fall of humanity. Isaiah also saw a glimpse of the Messianic Age when the Spirit of the Lord would come upon Messiah, and he would establish his reign. At that time of justice and righteousness, *"The wolf will live with the lamb, the leopard will lie down with the goat, the calf and the lion and the yearling together, and a little child will lead them"* (Is 11:6).

This is what Ezekiel was seeing when he heard the Lord saying, *"They will know that I am the Lord, when I break the bars of their yoke and rescue them from the hands of those who enslaved them. They will no longer be plundered by the nations, nor will wild animals devour them. They will live in safety and no one will make them afraid."* (34:27-28). God was renewing his covenant promises in the postexilic era when the redeemed community of the house of Israel would go back to the land under the care and protection of the God of Israel. This was a message that would later be declared among the exiles in Isaiah 44:26 where God says of Jerusalem, *"it shall be inhabited, of the towns of Judah, they shall be built, and of their ruins, I will restore them."*

37 ANOTHER PROPHECY AGAINST EDOM
Ezekiel 35

The word of the Lord came to me: "Son of man, set your face against Mount Seir; prophesy against it and say: 'This is what the Sovereign Lord says: I am against you, Mount Seir, and I will stretch out my hand against you and make you a desolate waste. I will turn your towns into ruins, and you will be desolate. Then you will know that I am the Lord. Because you harboured an ancient hostility and delivered the Israelites over to the sword at the time of their calamity, the time their punishment reached its climax, therefore as surely as I live declares the Sovereign Lord, I will give you over to bloodshed' . . ."

It is strange to find this chapter here with a prophecy against Edom. It interrupts the flow of Ezekiel's ministry to the exiles, and it would probably have been more appropriate to have been included in the prophecies to the nations, especially the prophecy to Edom in chapter 25. Biblical scholars are puzzled why the editors who preserved Ezekiel's words should have included this prophecy at this point. It may be that it was because Ezekiel was dealing with the situation after the fall of the Babylonian Empire and the return of the exiles to Israel, that it was felt right to remember the part that Edom played in the fall of Jerusalem by aiding the Babylonians.

Relationships between Edom and Israel had always been fraught with tension, and the way Edom openly rejoiced at the disaster that befell Jerusalem added significantly to the bitterness which was felt in Israel towards the people of Edom and Mount Seir. Mount Seir was the mountain range in the northern part of Edom's territory bordering upon Judah, and in this prophecy, they are treated as one nation.

After the fall of Jerusalem in 586 there was effectively no government in Judah following the murder of Gedaliah, and Edom took advantage of this by annexing most of the Negev, the area south of Beersheba. This infuriated the people of Judah who saw it as a cowardly act of terrorism, taking advantage of Judah's weakness and benefiting from her distress. This prophecy of doom against Edom would have been very popular among the exiles in Babylon who had already heard news of what the

Edomites had been doing, and how they actively participated in the looting of Jerusalem. This was certainly not a neighbourly response to the trouble that had engulfed Judah. The Edomites saw it as an opportunity to exploit their old enemy.

The antagonism between Israel and Edom went right back to the days of the settlement in Canaan when Judah was given the southernmost territory in the land, and the Edomites disputed this. David fought against them and subdued them, and his son Solomon, treated them even more harshly, actually enslaving them and using them for cheap labour. The Edomites never forgot this, and even though they joined in the conspiracy of 593 BC when they sent their representatives to Jerusalem to the meeting with Zedekiah and envoys from Moab, Ammon, Tyre, and Sidon, described by Jeremiah (27:3) they were never really friendly towards Judah.

This is what Ezekiel's prophecy is referring to in 35:5 where he says, *"you harboured an ancient hostility and delivered the Israelites over to the sword at the time of their calamity."* Their ancient hostility certainly went back hundreds of years to the time of David and the calamity referred to here is the recent sacking of Jerusalem by the Babylonians. As a punishment for this treachery the word of the Lord was that he would make the mountainous area of Mount Seir, a desolate waste.

The anger against Edom expressed in 35:10 was when the Edomites said, *"these two nations and countries will be ours and we will take possession of them"* – they were offending Yahweh, the God of Israel, to whom the land belonged. He had given it to the people of Judah with whom he had a covenant relationship and in taking this land Edom had given grave offence to Yahweh. Hence the statement in 35:13 *"you boasted against me and spoke against me without restraint, and I heard it."*

Yahweh's indictment was that *"at the time when the whole earth rejoices"* – he would punish Edom. The reference to when everyone was rejoicing was looking forward to the time when the Babylonian Empire would collapse and the exiles from Judah would return to their land and they would reclaim possession of the Negev which had been illegally annexed by Edom and Mount Seir. This pronouncement would undoubtedly have been an encouragement to the exiles in Babylon and it may be for this reason that this prophecy has been put at this particular point in Ezekiel's ministry.

38 A PROPHECY TO THE MOUNTAINS OF ISRAEL
Ezekiel 36:1-15

"Son of man, prophesy to the mountains of Israel and say, 'O mountains of Israel, hear the word of the Lord. This is what the Sovereign Lord says: the enemy said of you, "Aha! The ancient heights have become our possession." Therefore prophesy and say . . . O mountains of Israel, hear the word of the Sovereign Lord, this is what the Sovereign Lord says to the mountains and hills, to the ravines and valleys, to the desolate ruins and the deserted towns that have been plundered and ridiculed' . . ."

Chapter 36 represents a major change in the message and ministry of Ezekiel. It is the beginning of the turning away from the warnings given in the early days of his ministry when he was dealing with the sins of the people that had led to the exile in Babylon, and what he saw as the continuing sins of the people left back in the land. Ezekiel knew that in the justice and righteousness of God he would not continue to protect Jerusalem when it was filled with idolatry and the lives of leaders and people showed a lack of trust in the Lord. They were constantly breaking the first commandment of loyalty to God and as Moses had strongly warned the people – the consequences of breaking the covenant were severe.

Ezekiel had had to recognise the sins of his own family, the temple priesthood who had misled the nation by not teaching them the word of God, and also that Jeremiah, whom the priests hated, had been perfectly right in the message that he had declared. Ezekiel also had to recognise that the time would come when the glory of the Lord would leave the temple and depart from the city, leaving the way open to the enemy. He knew that it was his responsibility to prepare the exiles for the shock that this would bring. The exiles would be tempted to worship the gods of Babylon whom their Babylonian neighbours claimed were more powerful than Yahweh, the God of Israel.

Ezekiel had faithfully carried out this ministry, no doubt with many setbacks, but God had told him at the beginning that his task was to declare the word of God whether the people listened or not, whether they accepted the message or rejected it – he was to have a forehead of bronze. On one occasion God had told him that even the people in his own house group at Tel Abib listened to him but took no notice of what he was saying (Ezek 33:31).

One of the worst things that Ezekiel had been told to do was to prophesy a message *against* the mountains and the countryside of Judah that he dearly loved. The message was, *"I am about to bring a sword against you, and I will destroy your high places. Your altars will be demolished and your incense altars will be smashed and I will slay your people in front of your idols"* (Ezek 6:3-4). The whole land of Judah had been spiritually polluted by the people through their idolatry up in the high places originally set up by the Canaanites and either not destroyed by the Israelites or they had been revived by the people despite the strong opposition from their prophets.

Now the message was totally different. The first seven verses of this chapter are all introduction, culminating in the solemn pronouncement of God in 36:7, *"I swear with a lifted hand."* The message was the reverse of the message of doom Ezekiel had been forced to give. Now it was a message of restoration and hope for the future. *"The towns will be inhabited and ruins rebuilt!"* The whole countryside would be transformed, the land would become highly fertile and the people of Israel would enjoy the fruits of the land which will be their inheritance for ever.

This was a message of great encouragement to the people in the exile in Babylon, with the news that the day would undoubtedly come when they would be released and able to go back to their homeland. Many biblical scholars believe that this message was given just at the time when King Jehoiachin was released from prison in 561 (2 Kgs 25:27). He was not allowed to go back to Judah but stayed in some form of house arrest, but this, however, encouraged the hope that the exile would soon be ended.

Ezekiel's major message was that when the nations of the world saw the people of Israel back in their land enjoying prosperity, Judah would no longer suffer the scorn and derision of the nations. When the people of Israel were back in the land and enjoying peace and security, all the nations would know that the God of Israel had triumphed over adversity, and that he was again blessing his people.

39 DEFENDING THE NAME OF GOD
Ezekiel 36:16-23

When the people of Israel were living in their own land, they defiled it by their conduct and their actions.

This passage gets to the heart of the matter. It deals with the relationship between God and the nations, which was damaged by the people being driven from the land. Central to this is God's relationship with his chosen people, Israel. The people of Israel had brought the name of the Lord into disrepute in the eyes of the world because it was their sinfulness that led to God removing his cover of protection. All the world could then see that Jerusalem and the temple had been destroyed and the land was occupied by those who worshipped other gods, thus bringing the name of the God of Israel into disrepute. In the eyes of foreigners, God was unable to protect his land. So, the name of God had been damaged by the people going into exile.

The core of the problem was that they did not really know the God of the Covenant. At Sinai they had been given the Decalogue – a set of rules and regulations, but they had never fully embraced the Covenant as a living relationship between God and themselves. The prophets of Israel from earliest times tried to deal with this, and to teach the people that idolatry was a sin of rebellion against God.

Ezekiel hears God saying, *"when the people of Israel were living in their own land, they defiled it by their conduct and their actions."* The people did not realise how greatly they offended God by their worship of idols. God's reaction was to say, *"So I poured out my wrath on them because they had shed blood in the land and because they had defiled it with their idols. Their conduct was like a woman's monthly uncleanness in my sight."*

God hated idolatry! It made the people unclean, and it defiled the land that belonged to God so they could not have fellowship with a holy God. It created a barrier in the same way as a woman's monthly period stopped a man and woman having an intimate relationship. Verse 17 expresses God's repugnance of idolatry that alienated the people from him. This does not mean that menstruation is repugnant to God. It is part of God's creation and men also have an issue. Both are dealt with together in Leviticus 15 showing gender equality. There are no moral or spiritual problems with these natural functions which are simply dealt with by washing with clean water.

It is murder, violence, injustice, and the shedding of innocent blood together with idolatry which defiled both the people and the land. This is the reason why God poured out his wrath and scattered the people among the nations. He said, *"I judged them according to their conduct and their actions."* It was essential for the exiles to recognise why God had allowed them to be taken to Babylon. They were saying that God had not treated them justly, and Ezekiel was keen to defend the justice of God It was because of their own sinfulness that a holy God could not continue to be in a covenant relationship with them – they had broken the covenant and now they were bearing the consequences.

The people were grumbling about the suffering they were enduring through the exile, but they were not recognising the consequences of their actions upon God himself. His name was being profaned among the nations. The Gentiles were saying, *"These are the Lord's people, and yet they had to leave his land."* Ezekiel had no doubt heard Babylonians saying that Yahweh, the God of Israel, did not have the power to defend his own people or his own land. Marduk, the God of Babylon, was said to have triumphed over the God of Israel.

Israel's surrender in 588 had been a disgrace to the God of Israel as well as to the leaders of the people. The Babylonians openly rejoiced saying that their god was more powerful than Yahweh. The destruction of Jerusalem that had now happened – that no one ever thought could happen – was the height of disgrace that had been brought upon the God of Israel.

Therefore, the Sovereign Lord said, *"It is not for your sake, O house of Israel, that I am going to do these things, but for the sake of my holy name, which you have profaned among the nations where you have gone. I will show the holiness of my great name . . ."* The restoration of the land of Israel, when the people would return and rebuild Jerusalem and all the towns of Judah, would glorify the Lord God, who will show himself holy through his people before the eyes of the world (v. 23).

40 YOU WILL BE CLEAN Ezekiel 36:24-25

I will take you out of the nations; I will gather you from all the countries and bring you back into your own land. I will sprinkle clean water on you, and you will be clean; I will cleanse you from all your impurities and from all your idols.

In the statement we examined in Ezekiel 36:16-23, God announced that he would show the holiness of his name to the nations of the world. We will now move to the next two verses which form a prelude to the announcement of God's intention to put a new heart and a new spirit into his people in the exile. Before he could fulfil that promise he had to deal with the major issue that had caused him to remove his cover of protection over the land and to remove his presence from the city of Jerusalem.

The two greatest offences in the eyes of God were the shedding of innocent blood and idolatry. These two offences made the people dirty in the eyes of God – they were unclean and they defiled everything they touched. All human beings are sinners as Paul says, *"all have sinned"* (Rom 3:23), but not everyone recognises their sinfulness. In a cry from the heart King David recognised his own sinfulness and he cried out to God, *"blot out my transgressions. Wash away all my iniquity and cleanse me from sin"* (Ps 51:1-2). He knew that only God could wash away the uncleanness that clung to him like dirt on his body.

In my undergraduate days, as part of my training for ministry I served two years as the student pastor of a church in a mining village of Nottinghamshire. There were no baths at the local mine, and it was a common sight to see a grimy miner coming off shift with his head down hurrying home to have a bath before being seen in public. None of us likes feeling dirty, and as a nation we spend millions of pounds on disinfectants and household cleaning fluids for our homes, as well as soaps and lotions and cosmetics for our bodies so that we can wash away dirt and grease and appear clean and respectable before our friends, and especially if we are going to an important occasion or meeting people we want to impress.

This is how we should be dealing with sinful things that cling to us like dirt on our bodies. Only God can cleanse us, as David said in Psalm 51, *"Cleanse me with hyssop and I shall be clean . . . Create in me a pure heart, O God."* This is what God wanted to hear from his people who had disgraced him in the eyes of the nations. So he said that it was not for their sake that he was going to restore them, but so that his holiness would be seen through them by all the Gentile nations.

Ezekiel would have been used to people coming to the temple, offering an animal sacrifice as a guilt offering to cleanse them from sin, but in Babylon this was not possible – there had to be another way for sin to be washed away – through repentance and prayer. Only God could do this for his people. Paul recognised this when he asked, *"Who will rescue me from this body of death?"* The answer was that only Christ the Lord could wash him clean (Rom 7:24-25). Ezekiel did not know Jesus but he had learned to trust the word of God and if God said he would do something – it would be done.

It was at this point that Ezekiel heard God promising a great regathering of the scattered people of Israel among the nations – a second exodus and replanting in the land of Israel. Then, even more amazingly there came the promise, *"I will sprinkle clean water on you, and you will be clean; I will cleanse you from all your impurities and from all your idols."* Ezekiel had, many times during his training as a priest, watched the washing of animal sacrifices to ensure that they were clean and pure for an offering to God. If this was an important requirement of God, how much more important it must be for human beings to be cleansed from sin in order to be in a right relationship with him.

It was God's promise that he himself would do the cleansing and take away the impurities of idolatry. This was a wonderful promise that Ezekiel enjoyed relaying to the elders who came seeking a word from the Lord. They would all be able to go back to tell the people what God was promising. They were not far away from the Lord. God himself was promising to wash away sin, break down the barriers and renew the covenant.

41 A NEW HEART AND A NEW SPIRIT
Ezekiel 36:26-32

I will give you a new heart and put a new spirit in you; I will remove from you your heart of stone and give you a heart of flesh.

Christians have to beware not to use New Testament teaching in reading this statement, because the Hebrew understanding of 'flesh' is quite different. Throughout the Old Testament 'flesh' is used in a positive sense as part of God's creation of the body, all of which is good! 'Flesh' is not regarded as intrinsically sinful as it is in parts of the New Testament which is derived from Greek, not Hebrew roots. Even Paul uses it from a Greek perspective when he declares that flesh and blood cannot inherit the kingdom of God (1 Cor 15:50). God wanted to restore or redeem their human heart as originally created.

What Ezekiel is saying here is that sin (the shedding of innocent blood and idolatry) had turned the human heart to stone, so that they had become immune to the truth, and had refused to listen to the warnings God had sent through the prophets. He, the Creator was going to give them a new heart and a new spirit.

Ezekiel had now reached the central point of his message which no doubt he had been wanting to give for a long time. After all the bad news that he had been bringing, here at last he was receiving a good news message to give to the exiles. If we are right in dating this at 561, the exiles would have been in Babylon for more than 35 years. Many of the original exiles would have already died and a new generation born who had never known the homeland of their parents. Ezekiel's good news announcement would have been eagerly taken back by the elders to the communities in their settlements. But how would it have been received by young people who had never known any other environment than Babylon?

The answer to this question lies in the teaching that Ezekiel had been giving, that it was not only the sins of their fathers that had brought destruction upon Jerusalem and the land, but there was also individual responsibility for sin. God was now looking for each individual among the exiles to examine their own lives and feel ashamed of their disgraceful conduct, not only that of their fathers, but in their own lives. God wanted to get to the point where *"you will loathe yourselves for your sin" (v. 31).* The people would then be ready for God to fulfil his promise.

It was God's intention to put *"a new heart and a new spirit"* into each of the exiles, to create a new community of believers, each of whom had a personal relationship with the God of Israel. **They would be outwardly cleansed, inwardly renewed, and divinely empowered.** This continues to be his desire for his people today.

They would form the redeemed company whom God wanted to return to the land as a new exodus from slavery and there would be a new entry into the promised land. It was to be a new beginning for the house of Israel who would see the hand of God *"increase the fruit of the trees and their crops of the field"* so that they would no longer suffer disgrace among the nations. They would enjoy the fruit of prosperity of 'the land flowing with milk and honey' that was God's original intention for his people.

The new heart lay in the covenant relationship between God and his people in fulfilment of his intention – "*You will be my people and I will be your God.*" They would have no other gods and no other loyalties, and they would never again pollute the land. The Holy Spirit of God would be poured out upon them in the way that Isaiah would soon be prophesying – *"See, I am doing something new! . . . For I will pour water on the thirsty land, and streams on the dry ground; I will pour out my Spirit on your offspring"* (Is 43:19 and 44:3).

This would transform both the people and the land, and it would be seen by all the nations who had poured scorn upon the name of the God of Israel whom they thought was powerless. He will gain glory through his people and through them he will be revealed to all the world, which was his intention from the time he revealed himself to Abraham and set aside his family to be servants of God for the redemption of humankind. The redeemed company of believers – the Golah, would return to the land of Israel in triumphant procession preparing the way for the Messianic Age. As Isaiah would have said at the end of the exile, *"No longer will they call you Deserted . . . but you will be called Hephzibah"* (Is 62:4).

42 THE RESTORATION OF ISRAEL Ezekiel 36:33-38

"This is what the Sovereign Lord says: 'On the day I cleanse you from all your sins, I will resettle your towns, and the ruins will be rebuilt. The desolate land will be cultivated instead of lying desolate in the sight of all who pass through it. They will say, 'This land that was laid waste has become like the garden of Eden.' . . ."

In the previous verses Ezekiel described the cleansing of the people prior to their being given a new heart and a new spirit. In this passage we move from the transformation of the people to the transformation of the land, which had become defiled through the spiritual prostitution of the people who had activated all the old high places up in the hills of Judah where idolatry was everywhere including even temple prostitution. The report in Lamentations speaks of Jerusalem being unclean, *"Jerusalem has sinned greatly and so has become unclean"* (Lam 1:8). It was not only the city but also the whole land of Judah that had become polluted through idolatry and through foreign invasion.

This had been stated in verse 17, *"when the people of Israel were living in their own land, they defiled it by their conduct and their actions."* This is why this passage begins with God saying, *"On the day I cleanse you from all your sins, I will resettle your towns, and the ruins will be rebuilt."* Spiritual cleansing of the population was essential for the resettling of the land. The two were linked because the land belongs to God: he had brought his people to live there and their behaviour would have been seen by the nations of the world. Whatever they did reflected upon God and their behaviour had disgraced his name, so it was essential that they should be cleansed before re-occupying the land.

The pollution of the land after the people of Israel had been taken into exile in Babylon was further carried out by the occupancy of foreign nations coming in to possess land that belonged to Yahweh, the God of Israel, bringing foreign gods with them. This was part of the deep offence that Edom had committed. They had not only assisted the Babylonians in sacking the towns and villages of Judah, but they had actually annexed the whole of the Negev and much of southern Judah. This was seen as an offence against the God of Israel and a violation of his holy name.

The reoccupation of the land by the redeemed people from the exile would not only cleanse the land but it would also show the holiness of the name of God. *"I will show the holiness of my great name, which has been profaned among the nations"* (36:23). The transformation of the land that had been lying waste would be a sign to all those who had scoffed at the people of Israel and despised their God. They would see land that had been desolate for more than a generation, now looking as beautiful and fertile as the Garden of Eden. They would also see thriving towns fully inhabited and filled with life and vitality. These towns would be orderly and fortified showing the transformative power of God.

When the exiles were back in the land, they would cultivate what had been lying desolate in the sight of all who passed through it. This would be a witness to the power of God and would vindicate the disgrace that his name had suffered. All those who would see the land which God was going to replant would see what had been desolate and was now blessed with great productivity so it would yield an increase of fruit on the trees and of crops in the field (36:30).

The ruined cities of Judah would also be rebuilt, and their populations would increase as the Lord blesses them and they will become as numerous as flocks of sheep. They will be not be just like ordinary sheep, but like those who were set aside from all the rest of the flock for sacrificial offerings – each one had to be perfect. As the exiles coming back into the land as a redeemed community of the Lord, they would be set aside, like the sacrificial sheep, for God to use as his servants, bringing honour to his name.

We know from history as recorded in the postexilic books of Haggai and Zechariah, which were both written in the year 520 after the exiles had returned, that the people were by no means the redeemed company of the Lord envisaged by Ezekiel, and further described by Joel as those upon whom the Spirit of God would be poured out. This prophecy given to Ezekiel would not be fulfilled until after the coming of Messiah Jesus and the outpouring of the Spirit of God at Pentecost.

43 THE VALLEY OF THE DRY BONES
Ezekiel 37: 1-8

The hand of the Lord was upon me, and he brought me out by the Spirit of the Lord and set me in the middle of a valley; it was full of bones. He led me to and fro among them, and I saw a great many bones on the floor of the valley, bones that were very dry. He asked me, "Son of man, can these bones live?"

This is the pinnacle of the whole book of Ezekiel – the vision of the 'Valley of Dry Bones' and the miracle of resurrection it records. There is no date given for this vision but there is a clue in verse 11 where the exiles are saying *"our bones are dried up and our hope is gone; we are cut off."* This is a similar sentiment to Psalm 137, *"By the rivers of Babylon we sat and wept."* That was the sentiment when they first arrived in Babylon and the temple was still standing and Jerusalem was a thriving city. Here the promise is that it *will be established* (37:26). So this must be dated after the destruction of Jerusalem in 586, but before the promises of restoration in chapter 36 dated 561 – some time in that 25 year period.

We may safely assume that this remarkable vision was given soon after the destruction of Jerusalem when all the exiles in Babylon would be deeply grieving, not only for their relatives back in the land, but for what appeared to be the end of the nation of Israel.

What is being reflected in the statement *"our bones are dried up and our hope is gone"* is the reflection of the older men of Ezekiel's own generation who were born in Jerusalem. They were fearing that the whole nation of Israel was finished. They were the elders seeking a word from the Lord. They were trying to hold onto the teaching of their fathers and to teach the young people in the exile communities the history of the nation and their unique spiritual heritage as sons of Jacob, the years they spent in Egypt and the giving of the Torah at Mount Sinai.

The children of Israel had been rescued from slavery by the hand of God on that occasion, but now the nation had been scattered across the lands of Assyria and Babylon and there appeared to be no hope of a future. Their children and their children's children were already becoming absorbed into the way of life of Babylon, the land of merchants. The destruction of Jerusalem left the identity of the people of Israel on the edge of extinction.

Ezekiel was spreading the desperate situation before the Lord. Then the Spirit of God brought a penetrating vision before him. It may even have been something that he had actually seen on the march from Jerusalem to Babylon when they had gone through a valley where an ancient battle had been fought, and no one had buried the dead. It was not a fleeting glimpse rather in the vision the Lord took him backwards and forwards among the bones so that he had to see the full horror of the dead bodies on the ground and its terrifying reality. This was a picture of the land of Israel that was strewn with dead bodies and there appeared to be no future for the nation. Then he heard the voice of the Lord, *"Son of man, can these bones live?"*

It was essential for Ezekiel to face this question because he knew that the answer in terms of human logic had to be an emphatic "**NO!**" It was utterly impossible, but as Jeremiah had discovered, *"Ah, Sovereign Lord, you have made the heavens and the earth by your great power and outstretched arm. Nothing is too hard for you"* (Jer 32:17). As Ezekiel watched in his vision, God instructed him to prophesy over the bones and say to them, *"Dry bones, hear the word of the Lord!... I will make breath enter you, and you will come to life."*

The '*Ruach*' of God – his life-giving breath – would sweep through the valley transforming it from a place of death to the delivery-room of birth. When he prophesied, this is what actually happened! An explosion of power burst into the valley, sweeping over the rocks and echoing across its sides with an ear-splitting thunderous noise for which Ezekiel could find no adequate expression. The Hebrew for *'loud noise'* is lamely translated in our English Bibles as *"a rattling sound"*! Surely only the British could so underplay the reality of what Ezekiel was seeing!! But this was only just the beginning of the release of the mighty power of God in the resurrection of a nation.

44 THE LIFE-GIVING BREATH OF GOD
Ezekiel 37:9-14

Then he said to me, "Prophesy to the breath: prophesy, son of man, and say to it, 'This is what the Sovereign Lord says: come from the four winds, O breath, and breathe into these slain, that they may live.'" So I prophesied as he commanded me, and breath entered them; they came to life and stood up on their feet – a vast army.

We have already said that to call what Ezekiel described as 'a thunderous noise'– *'a rattling sound'* is a very poor translation. He was describing an explosive sound that shook the mountains and echoed down the valley creating an ear-splitting shockwave. It was followed by the bones coming together and then flesh coming upon the bones, but there was no life in them. They were perfectly formed bodies, but they were lifeless until God breathed life into them as in Genesis 2:7,

For Ezekiel this was a picture of the nation reborn with all its economic, political, and social organisation in working order, but effectively useless for fulfilling the purposes of God. It was a picture of the nation that many people wanted – they wanted to be like the nations of the world who worshipped bits of wood and stone. Ezekiel knew that they could not fulfil the purposes of God to use Israel to reveal himself to the Gentile nations. The only way this could happen would be for the nation of Israel to be filled with the Holy Spirit of the living God.

If the nation were to be reborn without the Spirit of God they would simply be lifeless institutions – all in good working order and giving the appearance of healthy activity – but useless for the purposes of God. Could this be a picture of the church in Britain today?

This was the reason why God made Ezekiel go *'to and fro'* amongst the lifeless bones in the valley, so that he got a full picture of lifelessness. He had to recognise the magnitude of the spiritual change that was needed in the nation. He was now ready for the message of resurrection that God wanted to give to him. This could begin the process of transformation among the exiles that would indeed give them a new spirit and a new heart that was essential for the redeemed company of believers who would return to the land and transform it into the cradle for the coming Messiah.

It was at this point that Ezekiel was commanded to prophesy again, *"Come from the four winds, O breath, and breathe into these slain, that they may live."* So Ezekiel once more prophesied calling upon the Spirit of God to come upon these lifeless bodies and fill them with new life and power.

The life-giving breath of God swept through the valley – entering into each of the bodies of the men, who then stood upon their feet – a vast army! Israel was not finished! The nation would not die! The fear that the enemy of mankind had put into the minds of the elders of Israel was baseless. The word of God would prevail!

When God makes a promise, he will always fulfil it. When he declares that he will do something – it will be done! That which appears utterly impossible to the human mind is easily accomplished by God. As Jeremiah rightly said, "*Nothing is too hard for you!*" (Jer 32:17). The resurrection of Israel from the ashes of Jerusalem and the scattered people of Babylon was assured.

Ezekiel heard the Lord say, *"O my people, I am going to open your graves and bring you up from them; I will bring you back to the land of Israel. Then you, my people, will know that I am the Lord."* This was the assurance that the elders of Israel sitting at Ezekiel's feet had longed to hear – that God had not finished with Israel. He was still calling them *"My people"*. He still loved them and was promising not simply to take them back to the land but also to raise them from the dead! The people who had wept beside the rivers of Babylon were going to be raised from the dead. God was promising a resurrection! The nation would be reborn, redeemed, purified, born again!

'Can a country be born in a day?' was the question Isaiah asked (Is 66:8). It was answered in the vision given to Ezekiel with an emphatic '***YES***'. That was repeated in 1948 some 2500 years later when the State of Israel was created over-night. God had not forgotten his ancient people, or this promise to unite them with the believers in Jesus "*to create in himself one new man out of the two, thus making peace*" (Eph 2:15). God's promises sometimes take a long time, but they last for ever.

45 ONE NATION OUT OF TWO Ezekiel 37:15-23

The word of the Lord came to me: "Son of man, take a stick of wood and write on it, 'Belonging to Judah and the Israelites associated with him'. Then take another stick of wood and write on it, 'Ephraim's stick, belonging to Joseph and all the house of Israel associated with him'. Join them together into one stick so that they will become one in your hand . . ."

This is another symbolic action oracle, a kind of 'enacted parable' that all the prophets of Israel used from time to time. Isaiah was told to take off his clothes and sandals and go around the streets of Jerusalem stripped and barefoot as a sign of what would happen to those who put their trust in Egypt to deliver them from the Assyrians (Is 20:2-6). Jeremiah was told to make a yoke out of straps and crossbars and put it on his neck to warn the people of Jerusalem of the slavery that awaited them if they went ahead with the conspiracy to revolt against Babylon (Jer 27:2).

Ezekiel is told to take a stick of wood and write on it the name of 'Judah', and then he is told to take another stick and write on it the name of 'Joseph' and all the house of Israel associated with him. The two sticks, representing the northern and the southern kingdoms are to be joined together so that they become one stick in Ezekiel's hand. He was then to hold this one stick in front of the eyes of the people and declare the message that God was going to select from all the scattered people of both kingdoms those whom he would take to the land of Israel that he had given to their fathers.

It was God's intention to unite Israel and Judah as one nation. Never again would there be two nations, or any division into two kingdoms. It had always been against the will of God that the division should have taken place. In God's eyes the division was the result of sin and should never have happened. There was always hostility between the two kingdoms and many times this hostility broke out into war, and many in the opposing tribes were killed or were reduced to slavery.

The northern kingdom had even set up its own sanctuary at Bethel which was described as *"the king's sanctuary and the temple of the kingdom"* against which the prophet Amos thundered and incurred the wrath of Amaziah the priest (Amos 7:13). Israel had been overrun by the Assyrians in 722 and many of its population had been scattered around different parts of the Assyrian empire. Then 120 years later Jerusalem had fallen to the Babylonians and a large part of their population had been distributed in settlements around the Babylonian Empire. There was no knowledge of the fate of the people from Israel who by now had largely lost their identity, but the exiles from Judah held together and formed a distinctive minority population. Much of the building together of the settlements around Babylon must be credited to the work of Ezekiel and his tireless ministry of teaching the elders, and in insisting upon Sabbath observance and establishing the Synagogue and its traditions.

The vision now being given to Ezekiel was for the return to the land of Israel – not only of the people of Judah, but of those from Ephraim as well. They were to become one united people, and God would raise up from among them a king from David's line who would be a true shepherd of the people. They would live together in the land as brothers and sisters of the same heritage on land given to their fathers, where they would live for ever.

This was a vision that had been given to Jeremiah even before the destruction of Jerusalem, that Israel and Judah would be united and restored to the land as one people under God (Jer 30 and 31). He received a word from the Lord, *"The days are coming, declares the Lord, when I will bring my people Israel and Judah back from captivity and restore them to the land I gave to their forefathers to possess"* (Jer 30:3). This coming together of Israel and Judah was central to Jeremiah's ministry and he foresaw God establishing *"a new covenant with the house of Israel and with the house of Judah"* (Jer 31:31).

This is what Ezekiel foresaw – the promise of God *"I will make them one nation in the land, on the mountains of Israel."* They would never again be divided into two separate nations. He would cleanse them of idolatry and save them from their sinful backsliding, making them one people and he would be their God.

46 ONE KING AND A NEW COVENANT
Ezekiel 37:24-28

"My servant David will be king over them, and they will all have one shepherd. They will follow my laws and be careful to keep my decrees. They will live in the land I gave to my servant Jacob, the land where your fathers lived. They and their children and their children's children will live there for ever, and David my servant will be their prince for ever. I will make a covenant of peace with them; it will be an everlasting covenant . . ."

This is a Messianic vision of the day coming when Messiah will come from David's line and be King and Shepherd over the restored nation of Judah and Israel. This will be at the end of the exile when God searches for his people scattered across the Assyrian and Babylonian Empires. Ezekiel sees the time coming when God will bring all his people back to the land where their fathers lived – the land that God had given to Jacob, the father of his people Israel. David, the ideal king who had been responsible for uniting the tribes of Israel and welding them into one nation, will be raised up as the servant of God to be their Shepherd and Saviour at the time of restoration.

Ezekiel sees that it was God's intention to establish a covenant of peace with his people, to cleanse them of sin and idolatry, as a mark of which God would allow the rebuilding of the temple so that his sanctuary would be among them for ever – he would be their God and they would be his people. This would be a sign to the Gentile nations that Israel was different from all the nations of the world – they would be 'holy' – separated from the practices of the other nations. This separation had been a requirement since the time the covenant was established at Sinai.

Moses reaffirmed the requirements of the covenant at the end of his life. He said *"See, I set before you today life and prosperity, death and destruction. For I command you today to love the Lord your God, to walk in his ways, and to keep his commands, decrees and laws; then you will live and increase, and the Lord your God will bless you in the land you are entering to possess"* (Deut 30:15-16).

It is part of the tragic history of the people of Israel that they did not follow the teaching of Moses, rather they embraced the idolatry of the Canaanites and other people in the land, despite a succession of prophets calling them back to put their trust in the God of Israel and in him only. By the time of Jeremiah, the threat of the nation being destroyed by foreign invasion was so great that Jeremiah wept. *"Oh, my anguish, my anguish! I writhe in pain. Oh, the agony of my heart! My heart pounds within me, I cannot keep silent. For I have heard the sound of the trumpet; I have heard the battle cry"* (Jer 4:19).

The disaster Jeremiah foresaw had now happened and Ezekiel was picking up the pieces in Babylon, trying to teach the elders who would each teach members of their community and now the end of the exile was drawing closer. He was hearing God speaking about the return of his people to the land. God was promising to cleanse the remnant of his people from the sins of their fathers, and of their own generation, by making a new covenant with them as Jeremiah had foreseen – *"The time is coming, declares the Lord, when I will make a new covenant with the house of Israel and with the house of Judah"* (Jer 31:31).

Ezekiel sees this new covenant as a covenant of peace, which would be an everlasting covenant that would be sealed by God dwelling among his people in the land that he had set apart for his covenant people. *"I will put my sanctuary among them for ever. My dwelling-place will be with them."* This is the first mention of the rebuilding of the temple that would be of special significance to Ezekiel as the place where he had spent his childhood and trained for the priesthood. The temple as signifying the presence of God and his blessing upon the people of Israel would be of enormous significance.

All the nations will recognise the presence of the Lord among his people, which will be the fulfilment of his purposes in calling the people of Israel to be his servant through whom he will reveal his nature and purposes to the world. This is what Ezekiel foresees for the coming of the Messianic Age for which we had to wait until the birth of Jesus to see its fulfilment.

47 REVIEW AND OVERVIEW OF EZEKIEL
38 – 39 and 40 – 48

We have now reached the point where Ezekiel has completed his task of saving the exiles from the depths of despair and they were beginning to reach the point of repentance which he had prophesied, whereby they would hate themselves for the sins which had led to God removing his cover of protection and allowing the exile to Babylon to begin. We have also had the beautiful message of chapters 34 – 37 whereby God not only forgives the sins of his people but washes them clean so that they can be in a new covenant relationship with him, the holy God.

Ezekiel now moves towards the climax of his message, presenting the vision of the new temple, the new Jerusalem, and the new people of faith, through whom God will fulfil his purpose of revealing his nature and his ways to all the world through his servant, the people of Israel.

Before he can reveal that vision of the whole of humanity being reconciled to God and living in peace and harmony with each other and the world of nature (similar to the vision presented in Isaiah 2 and Micah 4), God has to deal with those who are implacably opposed to the values of the kingdom of God, who hate his people Israel and are haters of truth and haters of God. This is what is presented in chapters 38 and 39. This final battle will not be for Israel to accomplish – God himself intervenes in the history of humanity and deals with those who cannot be changed by human endeavour.

There is a key verse in this passage that enables us to understand the purposes of God in chapters 38 and 39. It is the statement in 38:17 in which God asks a rhetorical question. The NIV reads, *"This is what the Sovereign Lord says: are you not the one I spoke of in former days by my servants the prophets of Israel?"* This implies the answer, "Yes!" But the NIV has wrongly inserted the word 'not' which is not in the Hebrew text. The Authorised Version is correct and so is the NRSV saying, *"Are you he one of whom I spoke in former days?"* which implies the response, *"No!"*.

This alters the whole sense of this chapter. If we follow the original Hebrew text, what Ezekiel is saying is that this attack by Gog upon

Israel is something entirely new. It is not like anything spoken of by Israel's prophets in former days. In fact, there is no mention of Gog anywhere else in the Bible, except in the Book of Revelation in the New Testament. Gog is not mentioned in any of the historical books of what we know as the Old Testament. Moreover, the great attacks upon Israel coming from the North such as those referred to in Jeremiah 1:14 and 4:5, have already been fulfilled in attacks from the Assyrians and Babylonians.

The attack upon Israel foretold in these chapters 38 and 39 is something entirely new. They foretell a time when Israel is dwelling in a sense of security and prosperity, entirely unaware of an attack and entirely unprepared to deal with it when it comes. This is certainly not the situation of Israel's response to the terrorist attack of Hamas on 7 October 2023 from Gaza.

All the attacks upon Israel, foretold by their prophets, were allowed by God to bring judgement upon his own people because of their sinfulness – primarily through the social sin of shedding innocent blood (injustice), and the spiritual sin of worshipping idols (idolatry). The attack by Gog and his hordes, all of whom are deliberately not identified by Ezekiel, are motivated by greed and wickedness (jealousy and hatred). Israel is depicted as totally powerless to deal with this attack and God intervenes with the total annihilation of the enemy attackers. This is clearly an apocalyptic vision of an end time battle between good and evil, light and darkness, in which God finally triumphs over the wickedness of humanity that has for generations been defying the truth and shedding darkness across the world.

This prepares the way for Ezekiel to announce the Messianic Age, *"I will now bring Jacob back from captivity and will have compassion on all the people of Israel, and I will be zealous for my holy name"* (39:25). This accomplishes God's overall purpose of reversing the shame that Israel has endured and redeeming God's own holy name which had been damaged by the exile of his people. He would no longer be hidden but he would reveal himself, pouring out his Holy Spirit on the house of Israel.

Ezekiel then describes the new temple and in chapter 43 he reaches the height of revelation in describing the return of the glory of the Lord to dwell among his people for ever more.

Now we will resume our study of the text.

48 A PROPHECY AGAINST GOG Ezekiel 38:1-13

The word of the Lord came to me: "Son of man, set your face against Gog, of the land of Magog, the chief prince of Meshech and Tubal; prophesy against him and say, 'This is what the Sovereign Lord says: I am against you, O Gog, chief prince of Meshech and Tubal . . . You will say, "I will invade a land of unwalled villages; I will attack a peaceful and unsuspecting people – all of them living without walls and without gates and bars" . . .' "

The two chapters Ezekiel 38 and 39 form a single unit in Ezekiel's ministry. They present considerable textual difficulties for biblical scholars, leaving many translation and interpretation problems unresolved. Prophecies of a great enemy coming against the people of Israel from the North had been made long before Ezekiel's time. The first recorded conversation between God and Jeremiah included him seeing a disaster coming from the North when an enemy would be *"poured out on all who live in the land"* (Jer 1:14). The enemy would come from an unnamed northern kingdom, although this could have been the Babylonians, who always came to Israel from the North.

Jeremiah had a further warning from God saying, *"I am bringing disaster from the north; even terrible destruction"* (Jer 4:6). This warning was repeated with a call to prepare for battle. There was an urgent need for the people to recognise the danger. *"Flee for safety . . . Raise the signal over Beth Hakkerem! For disaster looms out of the north, even terrible destruction"* (Jer 6:1). Many biblical scholars, however, believe that Jeremiah was referring to an invasion of Scythians that was threatened in the early days of Jeremiah's ministry, around 620.

Zephaniah who, like Jeremiah, had prophesied in Jerusalem in the time of King Josiah and whose ministry may have been familiar to Ezekiel in his boyhood, prophesied a great day of the Lord which would be a day of wrath and distress and anguish – *"a day of trouble and ruin, a day of darkness and gloom"* (Zeph 1:15).

Chapters 38 and 39 deal with unfulfilled prophecies, and today they are recognised for their eschatological significance. The prophecies of Jeremiah and Ezekiel that Israel would be restored,

Jerusalem and the temple rebuilt, were all fulfilled during the time of the prophet Haggai in 520. The first group of the Golah had returned to the land some 15 years earlier when they had given a free-will offering to pay for the rebuilding of the temple, but their top priority had been building their own houses. They had not done anything about rebuilding the temple or even the walls of Jerusalem. It was a disgrace that the decrepit state of Jerusalem was to be seen by all the surrounding nations.

Haggai berated them severely; *"Is it a time for you yourselves to be living in your panelled houses, while this house remains a ruin?"* (Hag 1:4). He said that all the troubles they were experiencing in the economy and in harvesting their food were because they had not put God in the centre of the life of the nation. It was God who had withheld the rain and caused the drought on the fields, resulting in poor harvests. He called upon the people to come together and begin work on rebuilding the temple. The people responded, building the Second Temple – although nothing like the size of the temple envisaged by Ezekiel.

That temple was destroyed in 70 AD some 40 years after the crucifixion and resurrection of Jesus. Following the Bar Kochba revolt in 135 AD the Romans carried out a further desolation of Jerusalem and widespread slaughter of the population, driving Jews out of the land and renaming Jerusalem 'Aelia Capitolina'. The land of Judah they called 'Palestine', 'land of the Philistines', as a final insult to the Jews.

In recent years we have witnessed the second restoration of Israel following the 1948 United Nations resolution, recognising the State of Israel. We cannot say that all the citizens of Israel today live in safety, but they certainly do live in unwalled cities, apart from Jerusalem. It was thought that they had the finest intelligence services in the world until they were taken completely by surprise in the terrorist attack upon a kibbutz and a music festival in southern Israel in October 2023.

This certainly was "*a peaceful and unsuspecting people – all of them living without walls and without gates and bars*" (38:11). However, it would be quite wrong to say that Ezekiel's prophecy is being fulfilled today. We can, nevertheless, say that Ezekiel foresaw times of great turmoil lying ahead for Israel, when they would have a multitude of nations against them, which is certainly true of the whole Arab world and parts of the Western nations where anti-Semitism is strong.

49 THE HOT ANGER OF GOD Ezekiel 38:14-23

Therefore, son of man, prophesy and say to Gog: "This is what the Sovereign Lord says: In that day, when my people Israel are living in safety, will you not take notice of it? You will come from your place in the far north, you and many nations with you . . ."

The second part of chapter 38 continues the theme of an attack upon Israel but now the attention turns from being solely upon Gog. The attack now comes from Gog and Magog. They have never been clearly identified, although most biblical scholars believe them to be located in the region around Turkey and Afghanistan. In 38:4-5 it was said that God would force Gog and Magog to attack Israel and they would be joined by a number of other nations, which can be identified as Iraq, Iran, and Sudan, together with others from the far North. That was reversed in 38:13, which says that the attack upon Israel will be a scheme designed by the attackers, Sheba, Dedan and Tarshish – thought to be Yemen, Saudi Arabia, and Lebanon. They will all join in because Israel is thought to be rich and prosperous and therefore there would be a great deal of plunder.

This apparent discrepancy between God forcing the nations and their exercise of free will, is simply an example of the way the prophets of Israel traditionally use the sovereignty of God. They often do not distinguish between the direct will of God and the allowable will of God, because in their view everything that happens is part of God working out his purposes for the world.

The attack upon Israel from an unnamed enemy is said to be an evil scheme they will devise. *"You will say, I will invade the land of unwalled villages; I will attack a peaceful and unsuspecting people – all of them living without walls and without gates and bars."* (v. 11) This attack upon Israel is said to provoke the anger of God who will send a great earthquake upon the land of Israel that will shake everyone and all creatures. Even the mountains will be overturned and there will be such confusion that no one will know who they are fighting.

To add to the confusion, God will pour out torrents of rain, hail-stones and burning sulphur on the aggressors. This will create enormous confusion among those mounting the attack. *"Every man's sword will be against his brother."* The combination of disturbances in nature and the violent weather patterns will be seen by all the nations of the world as a demonstration of the power of God – the God of Creation who is also the God of Israel, which will show his 'greatness and holiness' and will be part of God making himself known to the nations. This is said to be a demonstration of the power of God and his 'holiness' or difference from all of humanity. The outcome of these actions through which God will make himself known in the sight of the nations is, *"Then they will know that I am the Lord."*

Ezekiel is not the only one of the prophets of Israel to speak in eschatological terms of a great battle of the nations involving Israel. It is important to note that Ezekiel had just begun speaking about the days ahead when the people of Israel in exile would return to the land. God was promising to make a 'new covenant of peace' with them so that they would be living in safety and the land would become prosperous again (34:25-28). This picture of prosperity and tranquillity does not last.

Ezekiel foresees an attack from those who were the enemies of Israel and were opposed to what God was doing through his people. He says in 38:16, "*You will advance against my people Israel like a cloud that covers the land.*" Once again Gog is in the centre of this episode and the hot anger of God will be aroused. He says, *"In my zeal and fiery wrath I declare that at that time there shall be a great earthquake in the land of Israel."* He says that all the people on the face of the earth will tremble at the presence of God.

This is similar to the prophecy given by Haggai soon after the return of the Golah to the land. He prophesied *"In a little while I will once more shake the heavens and the earth, the sea and the dry land. I will shake all nations"* (Hag 2:6). The great conflict that Ezekiel was foreseeing was in the midst of a time of great confusion, with nations fighting against each other, and great plagues and bloodshed. God would be using this to execute his judgement upon the nations through this he would show his greatness and his holiness.

50 THE DESTRUCTION OF GOG AND MAGOG
Ezekiel 39:1-8

Son of man, prophesy against Gog and say; "This is what the Sovereign Lord says: I am against you, O Gog, chief prince of Meshech and Tubal. I will turn you around and drag you along . . ."

Chapter 39 continues the theme of a great war against Israel. The attack upon Israel comes not only from the far North but also from other unnamed nations. There are no nations named in this chapter other than Gog and Magog. Their identity has been the subject of speculation among biblical scholars for generations. Magog is named in one of the table of nations listed in Genesis 10:2 as one of the sons of Japheth, together with Gomer, Madai, Javan, Tubal, Meshech, and Tiras, but there is no mention of Gog. Three of the names, Gomer, Tubal and Meshech are named here in Ezekiel 38 and 39.

The geographical location of Magog is unknown. There are even more problems in regard to Gog, as there is no other mention of it as a place name except in a vague reference in Revelation 20:8. There have been many attempts to identify Gog as an apocalyptic pseudonym for the Babylonians, or Scythians, but no one knows where either Gog or Magog were located and all we have in the Bible is the vague reference to a place in the 'far North'.

The major purpose of the great conflict foreseen in chapter 39, is that God will use Israel as the means by which he will exercise judgement upon Gog and Magog and others who *"live in safety in the coastlands"* so they will know the Lord. These coastland nations are unidentified, and no geographical location is given. The central statement here is *"I will make known my holy name among my people Israel."*

It is God's intention to reveal himself to the world through Israel. But he must first ensure that the people of Israel understand his nature and purposes. They had never understood his covenant, so they have never been faithful to him. Ezekiel's teaching was to enable the exiles to understand why they were there. It was not because God had forsaken his people as they thought; neither was it because he had been vanquished by the gods of Babylon, as the Gentile nations believed. God's intention was to do two things: to teach Israel to know him, and to use Israel to reveal himself to the world. This meant dealing with the sinfulness of Israel before he could deal with sinfulness of the Gentiles. In order to accomplish this, he allows the enemy to attack Israel.

It is God who forces the enemies to attack Israel to carry out judgement against them. He strikes the bow from their hands so that they will fall on the mountains of Israel where the birds and the wild animals would feed upon their slain. The phrase *"I will send fire on Magog"* is a term used by the 8th century prophets for the judgement exercised by God. It is used by Amos five times in the first chapter. Here it is used by Ezekiel as part of the purposes of God to reveal himself to the nations.

Ezekiel sees this as the beginning of 'The day of the Lord'. He announces, *"It is coming! It will surely take place, declares the Sovereign Lord. This is the day . . ."*

'The day of the Lord' is usually regarded as an eschatological concept that began with the 8th century prophets of Israel such as Amos and Isaiah of Jerusalem. Amos 5:18 is thought to be the earliest reference in the Bible to "The day of the Lord". He declares to the people in the northern kingdom of Israel, *"Woe to you who long for the day of the Lord! . . . That day will be darkness, not light."* About the same time, Hosea who was also ministering in the north – covering the last kings of Israel before the exile – prophesied a day of reckoning on Judah's leaders, and Isaiah who was ministering in Jerusalem at the same time declared, *"The Lord Almighty has a day in store for all the proud and lofty, for all that is exalted (and they will be humbled)"* (Is 2:12).

Following the conquest of Samaria by the Assyrians in 722 the Lord through Micah pronounced judgement upon the enemies of Israel – *"I will destroy the cities of your land and tear down all your strongholds . . . I will take vengeance in anger and wrath upon the nations that have not obeyed me"* (Mic 5:10-15). 100 years later when the Babylonians replaced the Assyrians as the oppressor of the nations, Jeremiah pronounced a curse upon Babylon: *"Before your eyes I will repay Babylon and all who live in Babylonia for all the wrong they have done to Zion, declares the Lord"* (Jer 51:24).

51 THE DESTRUCTION OF WEAPONS
Ezekiel 39:9-16

Then those who live in the towns of Israel will go out and use the weapons for fuel and burn them up – the small and the large shields, the bows and arrows, the war clubs and spears. For seven years they will use them for fuel . . . On that day I will give Gog a burial place in Israel, in the valley of those who travel east towards the sea . . . For seven months the house of Israel will be burying them in order to cleanse the land.

Ezekiel is foreseeing the day of the Lord when Gog and the people with them will invade the land of Israel but they would be defeated, leaving behind all the multitude of their weapons. They will also leave behind a great deal of plunder that they had looted, and their redundant weapons would provide fuel for the people of Israel for seven years. They would not need to gather any firewood from the forest because the wooden weapons would provide them with plenty of fuel.

The defeat of Gog would be so spectacular that it would be at least seven months' work for the people of Israel to bury the dead. There would even be a special burial ground for the fallen warriors of Gog. Verse 11 presents a number of difficulties for translators. The word for 'travellers' is better taken as a proper name 'Abarim' which was the name of a mountain in northern Moab overlooking the Dead Sea, as in Numbers 33:47.

Thus, this burial ground would not actually be in the Holy Land, but over on the east side of the Jordan and the Dead Sea. Thus, it would not impede any travellers going east and would not require them to walk over defiled ground where the bodies of Israel's enemies were buried. The name given to this burial ground would be the 'Valley of Hamon Gog' – 'Hamon' means 'multitude' – a word that was often used by the prophets of Israel for the hordes of Gentile nations.

Ezekiel foresees that the great problem facing Israel at the end of this great war of attrition will be the pollution of the land. It is said that the slaughter among those who attack Israel will be so great that *"for seven months the house of Israel will be burying them in order to cleanse the land."* In fact, seven months will not be sufficient for this cleansing and additionally, *"men will be regularly employed to cleanse the land"* while others will be burying bodies left on the ground. Some men would be employed to go through the ground identifying the dead while others would be required to bury them. The scouts going through the land would set up a marker beside a dead body so that the gravediggers coming behind them would not have to search the undergrowth of the land but would easily find bodies and take them to the 'Valley of Hamon Gog' for burial. The marginal note about a town called 'Hamonah' is quite unknown, and many biblical scholars think that it is an error that has crept into the text. We can certainly say that it has no relevance here.

The burial of the dead now reverts in verse 17 to the days immediately following the great battle that resulted in the slaughter of the army of Gog. The scene that is described here of bodies lying on the mountainsides of Israel is macabre. It speaks of wild animals and birds of prey all coming to the battleground and engaging in a feast of flesh and blood – of mighty men and foot-soldiers of the different nations involved with Gog. This gruesome scene is presented at the end of the description of the great battle that will take place in Israel when invaders pour into the land and are actually defeated by an act of God.

The severe pollution of the land has encouraged a considerable amount of speculation among biblical scholars, especially in recent years since the invention of weapons of mass destruction. Speculation has been around the cause of death and the possibility that what is being described is the result of some form of radiation from atomic weapons or germ warfare that might have contaminated the land.

The strong emphasis upon the difficulties encountered by the markers and gravediggers in their efforts to cleanse the land from pollution appears to indicate something quite extraordinary that has happened to defile the land. This has generated considerable discussion about whether or not passages such as Ezekiel 38 and 39 have eschatological significance and whether they have any relevance for us today.

52 A SHOCKING FESTIVAL ASSEMBLY
Ezekiel 39:17-24

Son of man, this is what the Sovereign Lord says: Call out to every kind of bird and all the wild animals: Assemble and come together from all around to the sacrifice I am preparing for you, the great sacrifice on the mountains of Israel.

Ezekiel enjoyed having the elders of the exile communities come to his home and sit with him. He would certainly have enjoyed going through passages of Scripture from the Torah and elaborating on the teaching of Moses. There were many times when the elders must have been more than a little surprised at the teaching he was giving to them and the visions that he saw. There were times when Ezekiel deliberately shocked them, such as when he told them that unless there were repentance God would take them out into the desert and judge them, or that they would never be allowed to go back to the land.

The declaration in this word from Ezekiel would have utterly shocked the elders. What he was saying was unbelievable! Surely, God would not say such things – that he was inviting every kind of bird and wild animal to come to a feast at *HIS* table – the table of the Lord God of Israel – surely not!

The incredibly shocking words of Ezekiel were that God was inviting all the birds of prey and wild animals to come to a feast of human flesh – the ultimate sin of humanity was eating human flesh!

Ezekiel himself was no doubt incredibly shocked when he heard the Lord telling him to make this declaration to the elders. Was it really God showing him this horror scene? He would no doubt have exclaimed, "Surely, Sovereign Lord you cannot mean this!" Some 500 years later the apostle Peter made the same exclamation when he saw a rooftop vision of a sheet being lowered from heaven with all kinds of unclean creatures and he was told to *"Kill and eat!"* He protested *"I have never eaten anything impure or unclean"* (Acts 10:14).

The elders of Israel were similarly shocked to hear this declaration – there has to be a mistake. God would never make such an invitation to his table! But Ezekiel continued, *"At my table you will eat your fill of horses and riders, mighty men and soldiers of every kind, declares the Sovereign Lord."* There could be no doubt – this was a declaration from God, so what could be the explanation for such a horrendous word?

The answer came immediately, *"I will display my glory among the nations, and all the nations will see the punishment I inflict and the hand I lay upon them."* It is God's intention to deal with all those who are implacably opposed to God, who despise the truth and who hate his covenant people Israel. He will draw them together in a great combined army, attacking Israel who are peaceful and unprepared, but God himself will intervene, striking down their weapons and on the mountains of Israel they will fall.

The people of Israel would go out to bury the dead but there would be so many bodies scattered around the land that the birds of prey and the wild animals would get to them before the gravediggers could reach them. It was for this reason that God gave Ezekiel this horrific picture, the whole point of which was to stress the terrifying fate that awaits those who deliberately defy God. *"I will display my glory among the nations, and all the nations will see the punishment I inflict and the hand I lay upon them."*

It was always God's intention to use Israel for working out his purpose to reveal himself – his nature and purposes – to the nations of the world. He had told Moses that Israel was to be a *"kingdom of priests and a holy nation"* (Ex 19:6) through whom God would be revealed. It was essential that the nation should know that Israel had gone into exile because of their sin and unfaithfulness, so God had hidden his face from them, removing his protection and allowing the enemy to overcome them. They had to be cleansed of their sinfulness, but it was God's intention to bring them back as a redeemed company of people.

The Gentile nations would see the glory of God through the way he treated his covenant people, demanding faithfulness, loyalty and righteousness – qualities that were part of the very nature of God himself. When his own people were unfaithful they became dirty and could not have fellowship with the holiness of God. They had to be cleansed which was painful for them but it showed the world the justice of God. They would also see his loving kindness and forgiveness to his people Israel and to all those who were in a right relationship with him.

53 THE GLORY OF THE LORD Ezekiel 39:25-29

Therefore this is what the Sovereign Lord says: I will now bring Jacob back from captivity and will have compassion on all the people of Israel, and I will be zealous for my holy name.

One of the major purposes of the great 'Day of the Lord' will be to display the glory of the Lord among the nations. An important part of this revelation is for the Gentile nations to know the reason why God allowed the people of Israel to go into exile in Assyria and in Babylon. An essential prelude to this revelation of God to the Gentiles was that the people of Israel should fully understand why the exiles of Israel and Judah had taken place. This is why Ezekiel was raised up among the exiles to teach the people in the community villages around Babylon. His preparation for priesthood made him an ideal teacher of the Torah, the history of Israel and the teaching of Moses.

The progression of Ezekiel's own spiritual life and understanding of God is reflected in his teaching recorded in the book of Ezekiel compiled by his team of followers. His life's work did not begin until he had been in Babylon for five years experiencing life among the exiles, the hardships of those days and the bitterness of those who said *"Our bones were dried up and their hope gone"* (37:11). Like Elijah, it took a powerful storm on the mountainside to bring the word of God powerfully into his life. This prepared the way for God to speak directly to him and to commission him as teacher, pastor and prophet to the people of Israel in exile.

Jeremiah had stated publicly that the exiles were like the good fruit in a basket on the steps of the temple, while those remaining in Jerusalem were like the rotten fruit that was not eatable. Ezekiel's task was to prepare the exiles to return to the land as a redeemed company of believers in the sovereignty of the God of Israel and in total loyalty to him. His first task, therefore, was to teach the exiles that they shared in the guilt of sin and of breaking the covenant that had caused God to remove his cover of protection over the land and allowed the enemy to triumph. It was essential for the people to have a spirit of repentance before the Spirit of God could be poured out upon them giving them a new mindset – a 'new heart and a new spirit'. Only such a radical transformation could prepare the Golah to return to the land and be ambassadors for God in the evangelisation of the nations.

It was not because God was powerless but because of the sinfulness of the people of Israel in being unfaithful to God that he had handed them over to their enemies. In demonstrating this by restoring the people to the land of Israel, God would defend his name, which had been damaged in the eyes of the nations who thought that the God of Israel was vanquished by the gods of Assyria and Babylon. The nations would learn the reason why the people of Israel had gone into exile in Babylon - it was because God had hidden his face from his people and deliberately handed them over to their enemies until they repented of their offences.

God was now saying *"I will now bring Jacob back from captivity and I will have compassion on all the people of Israel, and I will be zealous for my holy name."* God wanted to demonstrate that he was different from the gods of the nations. His actions now in overthrowing the enemies of Israel and raising up his people would show his power to the Gentiles. Israel also would learn more about their God who was going to *"gather them to their own land, not leaving any behind."* He would no longer hide his face from them, but he would pour out his Holy Spirit upon the house of Israel.

The eschatological nature of this description of the Day of the Lord in an end time battle in the land of Israel, inspired the postexilic prophets of Israel and their messianic prophecies. It has also gripped Christians since the days of the Early Church and its language is reflected in the book of Revelation where the words of Ezekiel 38-39 are echoed. *"Satan will be released from his prison and will go out to deceive the nations in the four corners of the earth – Gog and Magog – to gather them for battle"* (Rev 20:7-8). There is, however, a similar promise of good news, *"Now the dwelling of God is with men, and he will live with them"* (Rev 21:3).

54 THE VISION OF THE NEW TEMPLE
Ezekiel 40:1-5

In the twenty-fifth year of our exile, at the beginning of the year, on the tenth of the month, in the fourteenth year after the fall of the city – on that very day the hand of the Lord was upon me and he took me there. In visions of God he took me to the land of Israel . . .

Chapter 40 begins the fourth and final section of the book of Ezekiel so we are using the first five verses of this chapter as an introduction to the sector. Chapters 40 – 42 are quite different from any of the earlier chapters in the book. They present a vision of a purified sanctuary in the centre of a purified community at the heart of the new city. The glory of Yahweh, who had departed the temple via the East gate before the destruction of Jerusalem, now returns to the new temple to dwell among a purified people, where the presence of God is assured by holy worship.

This whole new section describing the temple complex in chapters 40 – 42 is dated as being given in April 573, that is 13 years after the destruction of Jerusalem by the Babylonians. Ezekiel has had time to develop his teaching of the exiles in Babylon, establishing the reasons why God allowed the disaster that no one thought could happen. He was now reaching the stage where he could build upon the spirit of repentance among the exiles that had followed their recognising that the sins of their fathers broke the covenant with God and caused him to withdraw his protection. They had also accepted Ezekiel's teaching that they themselves were part of a generation that had defiled the land that led to the disaster. He was looking for a time to come when the exiles would loathe the sins that had brought about their separation from the land that they loved and that this would pave the way for a purified community of believers to return.

If we are right in believing that Ezekiel was 25 when he was taken to Babylon, he would now be in his 50s and, judging from the incisive ministry that he was exercising up until this point, we can assume that his memory of the temple in Jerusalem would still be sharp. So he would be remembering the place where he had spent his boyhood and his training for the priesthood and this is what he would have drawn upon in the vision of the new temple that is presented in these chapters. The vision that is reported here anticipates the rebuilding of the temple upon the original pattern of the temple built by Solomon around 950 but with enlarged asymmetrical measurements to reflect the glory of the Lord who had returned to Jerusalem to dwell among his people in the new temple.

It is unlikely that Ezekiel would have had access to any documents showing the plans of Solomon's Temple so it is most likely he was relying on his memory. He wanted the new temple in the restored city of Jerusalem to be as close as possible to the building described in 1 Kings 6 which he may have memorised during his training for the priesthood, but he also wanted the new temple to glorify God who had brought his people back to the land. This was achieved by taking the original dimensions of the temple but using a cubit plus a handbreadth which was the distance across the hand at the knuckles. The cubit ran from the tip of the middle finger to the elbow – originally of the king – and this additional handbreadth would be an act of glorifying God.

The presentation of the second Temple in the restored Jerusalem is described in the form of a vision in which Ezekiel is taken from Babylon to the land of Israel where he is standing on what he describes as *"a very high mountain"*. This is clearly meant to be Mount Zion which is a reflection of the idealised holy place on which the temple complex had stood. In his vision he sees a man whose appearance was like bronze. The man was standing in the gateway with a linen cord and a measuring rod in his hand who acts as his guide.

The guide is clearly intended to be a heavenly messenger who gives a commission to Ezekiel with a message to take back to the exiles in Babylon. The messenger then instructed Ezekiel *"Son of man, look with your eyes and hear with your ears and pay attention to everything I am going to show you"* (40:4). This was what he was required to report to the house of Israel in exile. The vision was intended to convey an extremely important message from God to the people of Israel in exile.

55 A CONDUCTED TOUR OF THE TEMPLE
Ezekiel 40:6-49

Then he went to the gate facing east. He climbed its steps and measured the threshold of the gate; it was one rod deep. The alcoves for the guards were one rod long and one rod wide, and the projecting walls between the alcoves were five cubits thick.

Beginning at the East Gate of the temple Ezekiel was taken on a detailed examination of the building, its layout, and measurements. From the inside of the gateway, he was taken to the outer court and the rooms off the pavement that led from the gateway to the North Gate which he also measured, and it was exactly the same width as the Eastern Gate, as were its portico and decorations. He was then taken to the South Gate which was exactly the same. Most of the measurements are two-dimensional, only length and breadth, so we have no idea of the height of the building. The long cubit being used was approximately 21 inches, thus the rod was 10½ feet in Imperial measurements.

The East Gate was the first to be measured as the temple faced east. The three gateways were all the same size and there was a progression of higher levels approaching the nave. The Guide climbed the steps to the threshold which was 10½ feet long. The alcoves for the guards were 10½ feet square. The gateway was flanked by three chambers on either side. He then measured the vestibule which was 14 feet from east to west and 35 feet across.

Then in verse 13 he measured the gateway, from door to door, finding the overall measurements from the rear wall of the side chamber to the opposite rear wall was 43 feet 9 inches. Verse 16 refers to narrow windows which we know were there in Solomon's Temple (1 Kgs 6:4). The outer courtyards were described in 17-19; and then Ezekiel was led to the north and south gates. There was a difference here between Solomon's temple and the new temple of Ezekiel's vision. In the new temple he saw an outer court set aside especially for lay worshippers, while maintaining an inner court for the use of the priests.

From verses 38 onwards the rooms were specifically set aside for the priests, such as rooms for the preparation of offerings, where they were washed and prepared for burnt offerings on the altar. There were also instruments laid out on the tables for this work.

Of particular interest to Ezekiel would have been the rooms for the priests, of which he would have had particular memories. It is notable that he was told there were two rooms for the priests – one for the Levites who did the general maintenance work and one for the priests who had charge of the altar who were the *"sons of Zadok, who are the only Levites who may draw near to the Lord to minister before him"* (40:44-46). This was perpetuating the appointment made by Solomon after he had assassinated his rivals for the throne including officials who supported him. He spared the life of the Chief Priest Abiathar who had supported Adonijah for the throne. He was sent back to his family land at Anathoth in Benjamin (1 Kgs 2:26-27).

From the time of Solomon, the whole family of priests at Anathoth, including Jeremiah, were regarded as second-class. As Levites they were allowed to do minor duties in the temple on a rota basis, but it was only the High Priest's family, the sons of Zadok, who were allowed to minister at the altar. They were part of the Jerusalem aristocracy and enjoyed the same status as the group of leaders around the monarchy. This division within the priesthood between the priests who were descendants of Zadok and others known as Levites went back hundreds of years to the time when the kingdom split into north and south when Jeroboam revolted against Rehoboam and set up high places throughout Israel which were said to have been ministered to by Levites. In fact, Jeroboam appointed anyone who volunteered to be a priest regardless of whether they were Levites (1 Kgs 12: 31).

It is interesting to see that Ezekiel had not lost the values that he had been taught from infancy which he expected to be continued in the restored Temple. He was told that certain rooms were for the exclusive use of *"the sons of Zadok"*. Ezekiel's vision of God giving his people a new heart and a new spirit had not changed his attitude towards the priesthood. He had yet to receive an understanding of the 'New Jerusalem' and the Messianic Kingdom of God as seen by Isaiah who saw the temple as a house of prayer for all nations (Is 56:3-8).

56 THE CHERUBIM IN THE TEMPLE
Ezekiel 41:1-18

Then the man brought me to the outer sanctuary and measured the jambs; the width of the jambs was six cubits on each side. The entrance was ten cubits wide, and the projecting walls on each side of it were five cubits wide. He also measured the outer sanctuary; it was forty cubits long and twenty cubits wide.

The conducted tour of the temple continues in chapter 41 with the guide completing the measurements of the outer walls of the temple and moving into the inner sanctuary which he described as the adytum, or *"the most holy place"* which was 35 feet square. He measured the outer dimensions of the temple which were a hundred cubits square. The walls inside the adytum were plain with no decoration but inside the sanctuary both the floor and the walls were all covered with wood. The wooden walls had carved cherubim and palm trees on them. Each cherub was said to have two faces: *"the face of a man towards the palm tree on one side and the face of a lion towards the palm tree on the other. They were carved all round the whole temple"* (41:19).

We are concentrating on the 'cherubim' when studying the first half of this chapter and looking at the 'palm trees' in the second half. The significance of these cherubim has been widely debated among biblical scholars. Cherubim first appear in the Garden of Eden where they are placed by God to be guardians of 'The Tree of Life' so that no human beings can approach.

In Psalm 18:10 the cherubim are said to be bearers of God as he soared on the wings of the wind, and Psalm 80:1 speaks of God sitting enthroned between the cherubim. It is possible that the seraphs, referred to in Isaiah's experience (Is 6:2), were also cherubim. They each had six wings and were flying in the temple when he received his call to ministry. One of these creatures in Isaiah's vision flew to him with a live coal from the altar and touched his lips, signifying the removing of guilt and cleansing him for the role of ministry that lay ahead.

At the building of the temple recorded in 2 Chronicles 3, Solomon is said to have carved cherubim into the wooden walls and doors of the temple where they were overlaid with gold. Cherubim were still there in Solomon's temple when King Hezekiah and the prophet Isaiah went into the temple to spread before God the letter from Sennacherib. *"Hezekiah prayed to the Lord: O Lord Almighty, God of Israel, enthroned between the cherubim, you alone are God over all the kingdoms of the earth"* (Is 37:15-16). This indicates that the cherubim were part of the temple decoration at that time, which would have been about the year 720, soon after the fall of Samaria in 721.

Further evidence that the cherubim were still in the temple up until the time it was destroyed by the Babylonians in 586 is seen in Ezekiel's vision of the glory of God leaving the temple just before its destruction. He said, *"Now the glory of the God of Israel went up from above the cherubim, where it had been, and moved to the threshold of the temple"* (9:3). Similarly in the following chapter Ezekiel says, *"Then the glory of the Lord departed from over the threshold of the temple and stopped above the cherubim. While I watched, the cherubim spread their wings and rose from the ground"* (10:18-19).

The traditional role of the cherubim acting as guardians in the decorations inside the temple was where they were watching over the Ark of the Covenant which would have been remembered by Ezekiel. In his original vision seen beside the Kebar River he had seen living creatures similar to those in the ecstatic vision that he describes in chapter 10, which he identifies as cherubim each of which have four faces – the face of a cherub, of a man, a lion and an eagle. The cherubim are closely associated with the presence or glory of the Lord. It was the cherubim whose wings spread and rose from the ground as the glory of the Lord left the temple at the east gate in Ezekiel's vision (10:19).

In the vision described in chapter 41 Ezekiel sees cherubim in the decorations carved into the wood surrounding the walls of the inner sanctuary. These cherubim, each with two faces, act as a prelude to the return of the glory of the Lord that is recorded in chapter 43. Cherubim are well-known features of Babylonian art for which there is plenty of architectural evidence and Ezekiel must have seen them in many places. By the end of the exile cherubim had become linked with Guardian Angels which may have come from Ezekiel's visions described to the elders of Israel.

57 THE PALM TREES IN THE TEMPLE
Ezekiel 41: 17-26

In the space above the outside of the entrance to the inner sanctuary and on the walls at regular intervals all round the inner and outer sanctuary were carved cherubim and palm trees. Palm trees alternated with cherubim. Each cherub had two faces: the face of a man towards the palm tree on one side and the face of a lion towards the palm tree on the other. They were carved all round the whole temple. From the floor to the area above the entrance, cherubim and palm trees were carved on the wall of the outer sanctuary.

In this reading we are continuing the tour of the temple that Ezekiel was seeing in his vision under the guidance of the divine messenger who was his guide. He was drawing Ezekiel's attention to the walls of the inner sanctuary that were covered in woodcarvings alternating between cherubim and palm trees. We have already looked at the evidence of the cherubim acting as guardians in the sanctuary, and now we are looking at the significance of the palm trees. Palm trees were greatly valued in the whole region, particularly in desert areas where the dates were used for food and the date stones were ground into camel feed.

Palm trees were regarded as symbols of prosperity and blessing. This was no doubt the reason why Solomon had carved palm trees as decorations in his temple, the building of which is described in 1 Kings 6. It was Solomon's Temple that provided the pattern for the temple in Ezekiel's vision. In this tour of the new temple at the entrance to the sanctuary, the doors were made of olive wood with five-sided jambs. The two olive-wood doors were carved cherubim, palm trees and open flowers and must have been an amazing sight that Ezekiel would have remembered from his childhood. The description of Solomon's work in 1 Kings 6:35 says, *"He carved cherubim, palm trees and open flowers on them and overlaid them with gold hammered evenly over the carvings."*

The reason why Solomon would have put palm trees in the decorations inside the temple would have been that the palm tree was widely regarded as a symbol of prosperity and blessing. We first read of its miraculous power just three days after the children of Israel had escaped from Egypt and were beginning their trek through the desert. They were desperate for water but when they reached an oasis at Marah the water was bitter. Moses threw a piece of wood into the water and the water became sweet (Ex 15:23-25). The Hebrew text actually says, 'a piece of palm' and it may be from this that palm trees became a symbol of blessing. In Psalm 92:12 palm trees are linked with righteousness and were greatly valued for many different kinds of provision such as making date-honey or syrup. The leaves of palm trees were often plaited for making into mats or baskets which were a great blessing to tribes who spent much of their time in desert areas.

Areas such as those around Jericho, the city of Palms, where there were whole forests of palm trees, were considered to be greatly blessed. The branches from the palm trees were prescribed as a lasting ordinance for generations to celebrate in the seventh month the festival of Tabernacles (Lev 23:40). The practice of waving palm branches as a sign of rejoicing is carried over into New Testament times and it is seen in John 12:13 when Jesus was on his way into Jerusalem with crowds shouting, *"Hosanna! Blessed it is he who comes in the name of the Lord!"*, and waving branches from palm trees. It was about the same period that coins were minted with palm trees – some of which have been found in the ruins of the synagogue at Capernaum where Jesus preached.

The final statement in Ezekiel 41 is that *"on the sidewalls of the portico were narrow windows with palm trees carved on each side."* This massive building was said to be 500 cubits square. There are major questions regarding Ezekiel's vision of the new temple which remain unanswered. Did he really intend that these plans should be used in rebuilding the temple? The enormous building that he described was certainly not built by Zerubbabel in 520, and it has never been built since that time. It is of great interest to biblical scholars as to whether Ezekiel was describing a temple that has yet to be built in Jerusalem. Or is the true vision of the temple the 'community of believers'? This would be in line with Paul's description, *"we are the temple of the living God"* (2 Cor 6:16).

58 ROOMS FOR THE PRIESTS Ezekiel 42

Then the man led me northward into the outer court and brought me to the rooms opposite the temple courtyard . . . Then he said to me, "The north and south rooms facing the temple courtyard are the priests' rooms, where the priests who approach the Lord will eat the most holy offerings."

Chapter 42 continues the conducted tour of the temple buildings begun in chapter 40, with the man with the linen cord and measuring rod in his hand leading the way. This is a short trip around two outer buildings on the northern and southern sides of the temple. These buildings were specifically set aside for the use of the priests. Successively all the outer walls, East, North, South, and West were measured and the entire complex is said to be a square of 875 ft.[5] As noted in chapter 41, this immense structure has never been built and it may be one of the unfulfilled prophecies that may still lie in the future.

Ezekiel's teaching on the role of the priests and the sacrificial system are very important for an overall understanding of the sacrificial system in the Old Testament. The exile, following the destruction of the temple in 586 was a milestone representing the end of an era. There could be no sacrifices during the exile and what Ezekiel is looking forward to in this chapter is the resumption of these following the restoration of the people to the land and the rebuilding of the temple.

With the destruction of the temple the whole theology of the nation had to be reviewed. For example, on the Day of Atonement the priests in the temple were responsible for offering an act of atonement on behalf of the whole nation, in line with the concept of the corporate nature of Israel as a people in a covenant relationship with God. Some other way had to be found through which that relationship with God, broken by sin, could be ameliorated. This had to be through prayer, which played a vital part in maintaining their national identity during the time spent in Babylon.

Traditionally in Israel, all food was bound up with the sacrificial system. No animal was killed for food without part of it being dedicated to God as his due. No bread was eaten of which some

5 John Weavers, *The New Century Bible Commentary*, Ezekiel, Marshall, Morgan and Scott, London, 1992, p. 214.

form of first fruits had not been offered to God, and some form of offering was required when coming into the presence of God. This was stated when the three annual festivals were inaugurated – the feast of Unleavened Bread, the feast of Harvest and First Fruits, and the feast of Ingathering at the end of the year. It was stated, *"No-one is to appear before me empty-handed"* (Ex 23:15), a command that is repeated in Exodus 34:20.

Ezekiel's ministry was constantly emphasising the holiness of God – his absolute difference from the material world, his 'otherness' and this is the reason why those who serve him in the temple must observe and maintain that separation from the world, even in terms of the clothing they wore. In the rooms dedicated to the priests they were to touch *"the grain offerings, the sin offerings and the guilt offerings" (Ezek 44:29)* and these were the ones that they were allowed to eat, but they must be wearing clothes dedicated to entering the presence of God. These clothes had to be left inside the rooms and the priests must change into outdoor clothing before going into the public arena.

Of course, none of these requirements were relevant for the exiles in Babylon, but they give an indication of the teaching Ezekiel would have been giving to the elders that they would have been passing on to the people in their communities. It would have had an emphasis upon the holiness of God and the need to come before him with reverence and awe in their times of prayer. In the New Testament this awesomeness of God is reflected in Hebrews 12:28. The feasts and festivals marking specific events in the history of Israel were important for maintaining their relationship with God as well as keeping the identity of the nation.

Not all of these events were occasions for joy. The exiles would also have remembered the day Jerusalem surrendered to Nebuchadnezzar in 597 and the destruction of Jerusalem in 586 with mourning and fasting. These traditional feasts and fasts were important for maintaining the religion and identity of the people of Israel and many were continued after the exile, which is why it is widely recognised that modern Judaism, with no animal sacrifices, was born in Babylon. Christians would say that there has been one sacrifice for the forgiveness of sins through Jesus. That sacrifice enables everyone who acknowledges him as Messiah to be in a right relationship with God the Father. Jesus *IS* the Messiah.

59 THE GLORY RETURNS TO THE TEMPLE
Ezekiel 43:1-12

Then the man brought me to the gate facing east, and I saw the glory of the God of Israel coming from the east. His voice was like the roar of rushing waters, and the land was radiant with his glory. The vision I saw was like the vision I had seen when he came to destroy the city . . .

The measuring of the temple had now been completed and the guide who had accompanied the prophet on his journey around the plans for the new temple is still with him and takes him to the East Gate. This is where the presence of the Lord had departed before the destruction of the temple in 586. This was described by Ezekiel, *"Then the glory of the Lord departed from over the threshold of the temple . . . They stopped at the entrance to the east gate of the Lord's house . . ."* (10:18-19)

Ezekiel fell face down when the glory of the Lord entered the temple through the gate facing east. Then the Spirit of the Lord lifted him up and took him to the inner court, *"and the glory of the Lord filled the temple."* It was at this point that he heard a voice from inside the temple *"Son of man, this is the place of my throne and the place for the soles of my feet. This is where I will live among the Israelites for ever."* This is the word from God for which Ezekiel had been waiting since the beginning of the exile, but of course he knew that the promise was dependent upon the obedience of the people, that they would never again enter into idolatry and *deliberately* defile the land.

Verse 7b is a very poor translation in the NIV which says, *"the house of Israel will never again defile my holy name – neither they nor their kings – by their prostitution and the lifeless idols of their kings at their high places."* The RSV is a much better translation, *"The house of Israel shall no more defile my holy name, neither they nor their Kings, by their whoring, and by the corpses of their kings at their death."* The next verse refers to the offence they had committed when they *"placed their threshold by my threshold and their doorposts beside my doorposts, with only a wall between me and them . . ."*

Ezekiel was remembering the years he spent in the temple and the controversy due to the remnants of the old complex of Solomon's Temple which had originally been joined to the King's palace. Although a new palace had been built, the graves of some of the Kings of Israel had remained close to the outer walls of the temple. Many of the priests thought that this proximity to dead bodies defiled the temple.

Verses 10-11 reflect the overwhelming sense of sin and defilement of the whole remnant of Israel in the exile as they reflected on their recent history and all the things that led up to the disaster that had befallen the land of Judah and the city of Jerusalem. The word given here to Ezekiel is that if there is a strong sense of shame among the exiles then it would be right for him to make known to them the vision that he has been shown of the new temple and the arrangements of its exits and entrances – and the whole design, as well as its rules and regulations. He was to write these down and present them to the people.

No doubt Ezekiel would have done this at one of the regular gatherings of the elders coming to his home. He would have described the whole ecstatic experience that he had had with its promise of restoration which would be good news for the elders to present to their communities. But they also needed to ensure that there was a true sense of penitence amongst all the people, so as to ensure that there is no return to the idolatry that caused the exile. The elders needed to ensure that the whole community in exile were aware of the pronouncement in the Book of Lamentations 4:13, *"it happened because of the sins of her prophets and the iniquities of her priests."*

Ezekiel succeeded in developing a new theology during the exile, recognising the justice of God as well as his mercy and love. Ezekiel was then able to build upon the repentance of the people and seek to prepare them for the fulfilment of God's promise of a new heart and a new spirit. His ministry was to lay the foundation for the redeemed company of believers, 'The Golah', to return and build the restored nation after the exile.

60 THE ALTAR Ezekiel 43:13-27

These are the measurements of the altar in long cubits, that cubit being a cubit and a handbreadth. Its gutter is a cubit deep and a cubit wide, with a rim of one span around the edge. And this is the height of the altar . . . For seven days you are to provide a male goat daily for a sin offering.

The regulations for building the altar and for preparing it for use, together with the regulations that were given in the previous chapter, 42:13-14 in regard to the sin offerings and guilt offerings, are of great significance. In order to understand them we have to go back in the history of Israel to the regulations for the whole sacrificial system given in the Pentateuch. The whole concept of sacrifice was to create or to substantiate the relationship between God and the worshippers. The sacrifice as a peace offering covering sin, both recognised and unrecognised sin, lay at the heart of the whole sacrificial system.

Sins committed by individuals who had offended other individuals were seen as an offence to God. By confessing their wrongdoing and making a sacrifice to God, while at the same time returning what had been stolen or wrongfully appropriated, plus one fifth of its value, the wrongdoer would be exonerated as laid down in Leviticus 6:1-7.

Corporate sin was dealt with through an animal being slaughtered and the blood sprinkled upon the altar on all sides. The flesh was then burnt on the altar as an offering to the Lord by fire which in the earliest times was thought to be pleasing to God – *"a sweet savour unto the Lord"*. The food that was eaten at the common meal after the sacrifice was said to create a bond between the worshippers and God. The share of the common meal that belonged to God was given to him by means of a wave offering after which it was given to the priests. *"From the fellowship offerings of the Israelites, I have taken the breast that is waved and the thigh that is presented and have given them to Aaron the priest and his sons as their regular share from the Israelites"* (Lev 7:34).

In the passage we are studying in Ezekiel 43 the dedication of the altar provides us with an insight into the spiritual condition of the exiles who since the destruction of the temple in 586 had become fully convinced of the fact that sin had caused God to withdraw his presence from the temple and his cover of protection from over the city. They had been warned of this long before it happened. Jeremiah's letter sent to the people at the very beginning of the exile referred to God as having sent them to Babylon, *"This is what the Lord Almighty, the God of Israel, says to all those I carried into exile from Jerusalem to Babylon"* (Jer 29:4). Additionally, Ezekiel himself had been strong in teaching the exiles that it was their own sinfulness that caused them to come to Babylon and not just the sinfulness of their fathers. He rejected the saying, *"The fathers have eaten sour grapes and the children's teeth are set on edge"* (Jer 31:29) and he strongly emphasised individual responsibility.

The new emphasis in Ezekiel's teaching in chapters 40 to 46 on the regulations for sacrifices shows the influence of this teaching. The exiles were now well aware of their own sinfulness of which they were deeply ashamed. Ezekiel's teaching of the justice of God showed them that the Lord was fully justified in removing his presence from the land of Israel, due to the rebellious and idolatrous practices of the people of Israel. As a result of Ezekiel's teaching there was a new emphasis on the whole sacrificial system of postexilic Israel with a greater emphasis upon guilt and sin offerings.

This emphasis is reflected in what Ezekiel said would have to happen before the rebuilt altar in the temple could be used. *"For seven days you are to provide a male goat daily for a sin offering; you are also to provide a young bull and a ram from the flock, both without defect."* The blood from these was to be put on the altar as an act of atonement and cleansing. This had to be done for seven days and it would not be until the eighth day that the altar could be used for offerings that would be acceptable to God.

The blood of atonement became firmly established in postexilic practice in the religion of Israel from this time which no doubt prepared the way for the theology of the New Testament with the once and for all sacrifice of Jesus and his blood of atonement.

61 THE PRINCE AND THE SHUT GATE
Ezekiel 44:1-9

Then the man brought me back to the outer gate of the sanctuary, the one facing east, and it was shut. The Lord said to me, "This gate is to remain shut. It must not be opened; no-one may enter through it. It is to remain shut because the Lord, the God of Israel, has entered through it."

This passage begins with the resumption of the conducted tour of the sanctuary when Ezekiel is taken to the east-facing outer gate, which is shut. He remembered his experience described in chapter 43 where he saw the Lord coming back to the city and entering the temple precinct through the East Gate. Once again he had the same experience of awe and he fell face down in worship.

Ezekiel was told that this gate was always to remain shut because the presence of God will remain in the city for ever and it was the gate through which the presence of God had entered and it should remain shut to everyone with one exception, *"The prince himself is the only one who may sit inside the gateway to eat in the presence of the Lord."* He is the only one allowed to enter through that gate.

This raises lots of questions for us today, that have been endlessly debated by theologians and Bible students. The foremost question is, to whom is Ezekiel referring – who is the prince? There are no clues in the writing of this chapter, or anywhere else in the book of Ezekiel and any answer has to be speculation. It is most usually assumed that it has Messianic significance, because no human being would be allowed to sit in the presence of God, and he is the only one who is allowed to enter through that gate.

Historically the gate remains closed today and is the central feature of the east wall of Jerusalem that can be viewed from the Mount of Olives where it is quite an outstanding spectacle in the early mornings when the rising sun breaks upon it. The Messianic connection with this East Gate is so strong that all the three major religions of Judaism, Christianity, and Islam recognise the significance of this gate. The Muslims are so keen to prevent the Second Coming of Jesus that they have created a cemetery in front of the East Gate in the belief that the

Messiah would not walk over the bones of dead bodies which would defile him. So all three religious traditions agree on maintaining the rule that the East Gate shall remain closed for ever – or at least to the end of the age.

Ezekiel was then told to listen carefully and to address the rebellious house of Israel among the exiles to whom he was ministering. *"This is what the Sovereign Lord says: '. . . In addition to all your other detestable practices, you brought foreigners uncircumcised in heart and flesh into my sanctuary.' "*

Ezekiel was told to remind the exiles of the reason why God had allowed the Babylonians to destroy the temple: it was not just because of their idolatrous practices of worshipping idols. It was also because they had no regard for the holiness of God. This is a major element in the teaching of Ezekiel. He continually emphasises the separation of God, his Holiness, his difference from the whole of creation that he himself had made, including human beings. Although they were created in his image to enable them to have fellowship with him, and even an intimate relationship through the covenant that he had made, the difference between God and his subject people was infinite. The 'otherness' or 'holiness of God' was so great that he required that *"no foreigner, uncircumcised in heart and flesh"* was to enter his sanctuary.

In the New Testament this teaching on the 'holiness of God' is particularly seen in Hebrews. Hebrews 12:14 says, *"Make every effort to live in peace with all men and to be holy; without holiness no one will see the Lord"*. It emphasises that those who have bitterness in spirit, or are sexually immoral, *"or is godless like Esau, who for a single meal sold his inheritance rights"* will not see God (Heb 12:16).

The message on holiness comes to a climax with the comparison between the place of the giving of the covenant at Mount Sinai and the heavenly Jerusalem, the City of the living God, into which Christians are able to enter amidst *"thousands upon thousands of angels in joyful assembly"* (Heb 12:22). At Mount Sinai the voice of God shook the earth. He has promised once again to shake the earth and all created things so that only things of eternal value remain – where we will worship God *"with reverence and awe, for our God is a consuming fire"* (Heb 12:26). We should have this sense of awe every time we enter into prayer.

62 THE LEVITES AND THE PRIESTS
Ezekiel 44:10-31

The Levites who went far from me when Israel went astray and who wandered from me after their idols must bear the consequences of their sin. They may serve in my sanctuary, having charge of the gates of the temple and serving in it . . . but . . . They are not to come near to serve me as priests or come near any of my holy things or my most holy offerings; they must bear the shame of their detestable practices.

This is a strange regulation that Ezekiel introduces at this point. It is an invective against those priests who were Levites but not descendants of Zadok. It is generally assumed that Ezekiel himself was a descendant of Zadok and that he and his family were serving priests in the temple at Jerusalem before his capture when he was forcibly taken to Babylon. We know that in the history of Israel after Solomon had assassinated his rivals for the throne he discharged the priest Abiathar who was chief priest during David's reign. He was sent to his home territory at Anathoth in Benjamin and Solomon *"replaced Abiathar by Zadok the priest"* (1 Kgs 2:35).

The descendants of Zadok were still the high priestly family in Jerusalem in the last days of the monarchy when Jerusalem was destroyed in 586. Jeremiah was one of the family of Abiathar from Anathoth and there was strong animosity between the descendants of the two families. Jeremiah said,*"from the prophets of Jerusalem ungodliness has spread throughout the land" (Jer 23:15)* He pleaded with the people not to listen to what the priests were saying to them. "*Do not listen to what the prophets are prophesying to you; they fill you with false hopes. They speak visions from their own minds, not from the mouth of the Lord*" (Jer 23:15-16).

Ezekiel speaks of *"the Levites who went far from me when Israel went astray"*. Biblical scholars have generally interpreted this to refer to the time when Jeroboam revolted from Rehoboam and formed the northern kingdom of Israel, making priests of anyone in the population. The two kingdoms were always at loggerheads and often actually at war with each other. Amos reflects the view of the southern kingdom of Israel in his denunciation of Samaria, and Bethel the national shrine of Israel. But there is no suggestion anywhere in the Old Testament of the Levites being supportive of the northern kingdom of Israel. On the contrary there is plenty of evidence that the Levites were faithful to Rehoboam and to the kingdom of Judah and they were active in ministry. We really do not know what Ezekiel is referring to when he speaks of Levites going astray, but it certainly perpetuates the distinction between the two families of priests and reinforces the dominance of the house of Zadok – *"They alone are to enter my sanctuary, they alone are to come near my table to minister before me and perform my service."*

There are also regulations in regard to the garments worn in the sacred rooms which have to remain there and not be worn in public spaces. The priests also have to have their hair trimmed and they are not to drink wine in the inner courts, and only marry within their own class of priests. These regulations were clearly designed to institutionalise the distinction between the different families of priests and between priests and lay people.

The distinction between things set aside for religious use and things to be used for other purposes have to be taught to the laypeople to maintain the distinction between priests, and people. The priests themselves were not to have any possessions but simply to rely upon the food given them during the exercise of their priestly functions. All these regulations were a reflection of Ezekiel's own background and the values that he had been taught from infancy, but it would be quite wrong simply to dismiss them on these grounds.

Ezekiel's own theological drive was to teach the people about the holiness of God who could only be approached with a strong sense of majesty and awesomeness on the part of the worshipper. His own understanding of God came through his experience of guilt and sinfulness that he himself had been part of the priestly establishment in Jerusalem. They had openly rejected the warnings of Jeremiah that God would not protect the temple or the city unless there were repentance of the idolatry and faithlessness of the nation. It was a strong sense of guilt and sinfulness that lay behind his emphasis upon the distinction between the sacred and the secular and therefore upon the holiness of God in whose presence he had a strong sense of awe and before whom, he always fell face downwards in worship.

63 ALLOTTING THE LAND Ezekiel 45:1-12

When you allot the land as an inheritance, you are to present to the Lord a portion of the land as a sacred district, 25,000 cubits long and 20,000 cubits wide; the entire area will be holy. Of this, a section 500 cubits square is to be for the sanctuary, with 50 cubits around it for open land.

This is a fascinating little insight into the vision for the ideal restoration of the land of Israel at the end of the exile. Ezekiel believed it to be of primary importance to give the Lord his place at the centre of the nation. Giving God his portion has spiritual significance for the health and well-being of society and for resetting the values of the nation that had been so corrupt during the reigns of Jehoiakim and Zedekiah. It was during their reigns that idolatry escalated, and moral and spiritual values collapsed. Jeremiah's famous sermon preached outside the Temple (Jer 7), highlighted the disastrous state of the nation awash with injustice and oppression, violence and bloodshed, adultery and idolatry.

Putting God in the very centre of the nation's social , as well as in the centre of its religious practices, was a symbol of the 'new heart and new spirit' that God had told Ezekiel he would give to the redeemed company of believers coming out of the exile. In this vision that Ezekiel is given, not only is the sanctuary given a central location, but close to it also will be land for the priests who minister in the sanctuary. *"It will be a place for their houses as well as a holy place for the sanctuary."* There will be a similar area given to the Levites and their families who will be serving the temple.

Then there will be an area of land adjoining the sacred area that will be left open, belonging to the city, but not built upon. It will be an area for the use of all the population of the house of Israel. Alongside this open area there will be land allocated for the civic ruler. He is designated 'a prince' but this does not signify a resumption of the monarchy. It is simply a generic term for a civic ruler.

There is no indication of how the ruler will be appointed. We are simply told that he will have land allocated to him and that this land will be his personal possession. There is nothing to say how he can be dismissed or replaced if he fails to meet the standards that are set for his leadership. The emphasis is upon a change in the type of leadership that will be expected. There must be no more oppression, no more injustice from which the poor and those lacking in social status or wealth have traditionally suffered in Israel.

The prophet Amos did a brilliant job in summarising the injustices of both Judah and Israel in a superb speech to the people in the northern kingdom which gives a vivid picture of a corrupt society. He described; as a word from the Lord, the northern kingdom of Israel where, *"They sell the righteous for silver, and the needy for a pair of sandals. They trample on the heads of the poor as upon the dust of the ground and deny justice to the oppressed. Father and son use the same girl and so profane my holy name"* (*Amos 2:6-7*).

It is against this background that Ezekiel was reacting. He said, *"This is what the Sovereign Lord says: you have gone far enough, O princes of Israel! Give up your violence and oppression and do what is just and right. Stop dispossessing my people, declares the Sovereign Lord. You are to use accurate scales, an accurate ephah and an accurate bath."*

Not only were the weights and measures to be accurate, but the financial system had to be reformed. Justice was clearly to be established and maintained at the very heart of the whole social and economic systems of the nation as a requirement of the Lord. The redeemed community that was being moulded in Babylon in preparation for the return to the land of Israel had to have justice and righteousness at the heart of its life and this is what is foreseen in the vision given to Ezekiel in this section.

It was this emphasis upon justice and righteousness in the tradition of the prophets of Israel that became a central feature of the teaching of Jesus reflected in his parables. In Jesus' own prophetic ministry, he sounded very much like the 8th to 6th century prophets of Israel when he denounced the values and practices of the teachers of the law and the Pharisees, such as in the seven woes of Matthew 23.

64 AN ACT OF ATONEMENT Ezekiel 45:13-25

This is the special gift you are to offer: one sixth of an ephah from each homer of wheat and a sixth of an ephah from each homer of barley . . . Also one sheep is to be taken from every flock of two hundred from the well-watered pastures of Israel.

The second half of chapter 45 moves away from the divisions of the land and the social regulations required of the nations in the leadership in the post-exilic restoration. Ezekiel was well aware that not only had Jerusalem and all the major cities such as Lachish and Hebron been destroyed, but virtually the whole social and economic structure of the land of Judah had been shattered. The task facing the redeemed company of the house of Israel who returned to the land, would not simply be rebuilding ruined buildings, but be re-establishing the whole economic and social life of the nation including law and order.

Ezekiel was also aware of the need for total change from the old order under the monarchy and the establishment that existed in his boyhood of which he no doubt had plenty of memories. In Babylon he had unlimited time for reflection and re-evaluating the situation that produced the disaster that had happened. The vision he had received of the 'valley of dry bones' and the prophetic words from God promising a 'new heart and a new spirit' for the restored nation, convinced him that God's intention was for planting a radically different nation with his presence being central to everything.

Ezekiel's personal experience of the presence of God in his life and the ecstatic visions he had received that transformed his life, convinced him of the awesomeness of God and his holiness. This became the central feature of his teaching and Ezekiel was responsible for preserving the spiritual heritage of the nation and for shaping the religious observances of its feasts and festivals during the exile. His teaching provided the foundations upon which the whole future beliefs and practices of Judaism rested. An outstanding feature of his teaching was not only the holiness of God but the sinfulness of the nation. It was Ezekiel, more than anyone else, who generated the sense of individual responsibility for the sins of the nation and the desire to re-establish a right relationship with the God of their fathers who had chosen Israel to be his people.

Ezekiel taught the people that the breaking of the covenant with God lay at the root of their present situation and that the re-establishment of that covenant relationship was central to a successful re-establishing of the nation in the aftermath of the exile. This is what lies at the heart of this passage of Scripture in Ezekiel 45:13-25. The special gift mentioned here is part of the preparation for a national act of atonement that would be needed at the beginning of the re-entry of the land, after the exile.

This national act of atonement was something in which all the people would participate. *"All the people of the land will participate in this special gift for the use of the prince in Israel. It will be the duty of the prince to provide the burnt offerings, grain offerings and drink offerings at the festivals."* The purpose of all these offerings would be *"to make atonement for the house of Israel" (45:17).*

The act of atonement was to ensure that the nation was 'at one' with God, and this could only be achieved through repentance for the past and cleansing of the present. In order to achieve this everyone would participate, but the priests would have special responsibility for sin offerings to cleanse the sanctuary by using the methods described in Leviticus and already noted in Ezekiel 43:13-26. They would take the blood of the bull and scatter it over the doorposts of the temple and the altar and make special offering for any unintentional sins, or sins committed in ignorance, in order to ensure that the act of atonement was complete.

When they were actually back in the land, the first Passover feast would be a special celebration, possibly like the one celebrated by King Hezekiah who reopened the temple after the sins of King Ahaz. *"The whole assembly then agreed to celebrate the festival seven more days"* (2 Chron 30:23). At this special first Passover after the Exile there was to be an emphasis upon a sin offering. *"Every day during the seven days of the Feast he* (the prince) *is to provide seven bulls and seven rams"* for the burnt offering. The sacrifice of the bulls was to ensure the atonement with God in the same way as in New Testament times the sacrifice of Jesus on the cross ensured the atonement of those who put their trust in him.

65 OFFERINGS AND HOLY DAYS Ezekiel 46

This is what the Sovereign Lord says: The gate of the inner court facing east is to be shut on the six working days, but on the Sabbath day and on the day of the New Moon it is to be opened . . ."

This chapter continues the theme begun at Ezekiel 45:13, adding a number of rules and regulations for various feasts and sacrifices. Verses 1 to 3 refer to the opening of the inner east gate on the Sabbath and on New Moon festivals. They include requirements for the prince who is to supply sacrifices for the priests to offer. It is significant that all the people of the land are required to worship in the presence of the Lord on the Sabbath and New Moons. This is not something that happened in Israel before the exile. It was during the exile, after much admonition from Ezekiel that Sabbath observance became widespread in the exile communities. In Ezekiel 20 there are numerous references to the Sabbath-breaking that occurred prior to the exile and how the leaders and people utterly desecrated the Sabbaths which was the reason why *'God poured out his wrath'* upon them.

Ezekiel brought a word which he gave to the elders and was passed on to the people through them – *"I am the Lord your God; follow my decrees and be careful to keep my laws. Keep my Sabbaths holy, that they may be a sign between us"* (20:19-20). Keeping the Sabbath became one of the distinctive marks of the exile communities and their refusal to work on Saturdays was honoured by the Babylonians as one of the requirements of the God of Israel.

In this final part of his ministry, Ezekiel is outlining the regulations for religious observance in the postexilic nation where Sabbath observance had already become well established. The objective of all these regulations is to honour the holiness of God and to ensure that nothing is done that might contaminate the purity of the offerings made to God. This is why it is even important in verses 9-11 to regulate the entrances and exits for prince and people on feast days. Verse 12 regulates the procedure with the inner east gate for the freewill offerings of the prince and verses 13 and 14 provide for the burnt offering that should be offered morning by morning.

Verses 16 to 18 lay down the rules of inheritance for the prince and his family to guard against injustice and exploiting the people. If he wishes to give a gift of land to his son it must be from his own property and not by taking property from other people, but if he gives property away to one of his servants it has to be returned at the Jubilee. The inspection of the sanctuary is resumed in verse 19 led by the divine messenger and Ezekiel is taken to the rooms occupied by the priests. Inside the courtyard were the kitchens where the priests would cook the guilt offering, the sin offering, and also baked the grain offering. It had to be done in rooms where the public were not allowed, in order to maintain their sacred nature and avoid contamination of the offerings.

The significance of all these regulations is to guard the holiness of God which is Ezekiel's main theme. He has been made so aware of the reasons why God removed his cover of protection that his central focus here is to guard against offending God through polluted offerings. This became a major theological discussion among the exiles which was carried over at the end of the exile to life in Jerusalem where the Prophet Haggai discussed the issue with the priests (Hag 2:10-14). This was why Ezekiel had stressed the need for the elders to teach the people the "*difference between the holy and the common and to show them how to distinguish between the unclean and the clean*" (Ezek 44:23).

The central issue of all these regulations was 'atonement' – to re-establish the broken relationship between God and the people of Israel that had resulted in the exile. Ezekiel's task during the exile was to re-establish the covenant relationship with God, hence his emphasis upon guilt and sin in the offerings to God being planned for the new temple. Ezekiel had not yet understood the purposes of God to achieve atonement through the person of Messiah and so his whole attention was to use animal sacrifice as the means of establishing an intimate relationship of being 'at one' with God. Nevertheless, his understanding of the holiness of God is a valuable contribution preparing the way for the message of the New Testament and the gospel of the kingdom announced by Jesus and sealed by his blood.

66 THE RIVER OF LIFE Ezekiel 47:1-12

The man brought me back to the entrance of the temple, and I saw water coming out from under the threshold of the temple towards the east (for the temple faced east). The water was coming down from under the south side of the temple, south of the altar.

We come now to the final vision of Ezekiel's ministry. It concludes the conducted tour of the sanctuary led by the heavenly messenger who had been guiding Ezekiel through the new Jerusalem after the exile. The vision of a fountain of water arising from under the temple and flowing out towards the east is clearly linked to the promise of a new heart and a new spirit for the newly restored nation that was noted in chapter 36.

The man with a measuring line in his hand measured a thousand cubits where the water was found to be ankle-deep. A second thousand cubits revealed the water to be knee deep. Another thousand cubits and it was now waist deep. A further one thousand cubits reached the point where it was no longer possible to walk across the bed of the river. It was now sufficiently deep for swimming.

The message would no doubt have been a great encouragement to the elders in Babylon. Here was a message they could take back to their communities and share with the people. God was not only promising to take them back to the land of their forefathers, but also to renew the whole nation, including rebuilding the city of Jerusalem with a new temple at its centre.

The promise was that, from the new temple, new life would flow into the nation. It would come from the presence of God himself who had not forgotten his people. He would freely forgive them now that they were acknowledging their sinfulness and the sins of their fathers. God was promising to renew the covenant and his forgiveness would flow from the temple in an ever-deepening stream out into the life of the nation that would bless all the people. The blessing would be so great that as the river became deeper they would not be able to keep their feet on the ground but would have to swim and they would find that the water carried them. They would have to stop walking in their own strength and trust the Spirit of God who would transform their lives and fill them with new power.

God's forgiveness would be a sign of atonement – the re-establishing of his 'at oneness' with his people, and the cleansing power of the water from the temple would change everything through which it flowed. The land that had been desecrated by idolatry and faithlessness was now being transformed. This was no less than a divine act of re-creation of the land as the water of life flowed out through the east gate that would one day welcome the Messiah.

Everywhere the water flowed was purified, not only making the land abundantly fruitful, but transforming all life including the towns and villages. The transformation will be so great that even fish will live in the Dead Sea, while leaving the marshes for their abundance of minerals.

The miracle of new life will extend to the whole world of nature where there were not only fishermen fishing in the Dead Sea, but all along the banks of the river there will be fruit trees of all kinds. They will be so abundant that there will be fruit every month which will provide health and vitality and even healing for the people. The new life from the sanctuary will be at the heart of the newly transformed people of Israel cleansed and purified by the presence of God in the centre of the nation.

This picture of a river flowing through the land bringing new life is at the heart of the religious tradition of Israel. Psalm 46 speaks of the river whose streams make glad the city of God. In the Garden of Eden, central to the creation story, there were four great rivers flowing out to water the earth (Gen 2:10). Zechariah 13:1 sees a fountain opening to the house of David and the inhabitants of Jerusalem to cleanse them from sin and impurity. Then the Bible ends with the declaration of the River of Life, flowing from the throne of God and the Lamb of God, down the middle of the city street. On each side of the river there are trees bearing fruit for food and for healing. The final declaration is, *"Blessed are those who wash their robes, that they may have the right to the tree of life and may go through the gates into the city"* (Rev 22:14).

67 BOUNDARIES AND INHERITANCE
Ezekiel 47:13-23

This is what the Sovereign Lord says: "These are the boundaries by which you are to divide the land for an inheritance . . ."

Ezekiel is looking forward to the repossessing of the land of their forefathers at the end of the exile. We can be sure that he either had a copy of parts of the Pentateuch, such as the scroll with the part of Deuteronomy that was discovered during Josiah's repairs to the temple, or that he had memorised parts of the work of Moses in his training for the priesthood. Numbers 34 would have been part of this, where the boundaries of the promised land were set out. These are what Ezekiel has in mind here.

The division of the land noted here is roughly the area bounded by the Mediterranean Sea in the West, to the River Jordan in the East. The northern boundary is roughly on a line going westwards from Damascus to the Mediterranean coast, and in the south it is bounded on a line running from the southern tip of the Dead Sea to the Wadi of Egypt.

There is a lot of controversy among biblical scholars concerning the identity of those inhabitants described in Ezekiel 47:21-23. They are described as 'aliens' who are to receive an equal share of land together with those of the Golah returning to Israel from Babylon. The command here is, *"You are to distribute this land among yourselves according to the tribes of Israel . . . for yourselves and for the aliens who have settled among you and who have children."* This is an incredible statement showing a liberal spirit quite alien to the teaching of Nehemiah who would not allow Tobiah the Ammonite to share in rebuilding the walls of Jerusalem (Neh 2:20 and 4:3). Ezra told the men who had married foreign wives to reject them and their children, instead of teaching them to know the God of Israel (Ezra 10:11).

The question in this statement made by Ezekiel is, who are the 'aliens'? The usual assumption is that they are people from the neighbouring nations of Edom, Ammon, Moab and Tyre who had moved on to the pastureland of Judah following its destruction by the Babylonians when its villages were left unguarded. This would be a remarkable concession especially if expressed towards the people of Edom who had aided the Babylonians and rejoiced when Jerusalem was sacked. They, like Sanballat who opposed the rebuilding of the walls of Jerusalem in the time of Nehemiah (Neh 4:1), were certainly not friendly towards the Israelites.

Other aliens could have been those who had been settled by Sennacherib following his conquest of Samaria in 722 BC. Some of these aliens were included in those who gave their lives to the Lord during the great spiritual revival led by Hezekiah. *"The entire assembly of Judah rejoiced, along with the priests and Levites and all who had assembled from Israel, including the aliens who had come from Israel and those who lived in Judah"* (2 Chron 30:25). These would have been proselytes rather than aliens hostile to Judaism. They were those who had settled and had families, and they and their children had accepted the God of Israel as their God which put them in a very different category from Tobiah the Ammonite (Neh 4:3).

The land was to be divided equally between all those who returned to the land of Israel in accordance with God's sworn purposes made known to their forefathers, but in accepting the portion of the land, they would be coming under the same regulations as laid down in the time of Moses. This would certainly be in the mind of Ezekiel who regarded the land as a sacred trust with obligations when given to the people. This would undoubtedly have been his interpretation of 'inheritance'.

Moses had continually stressed that the land was linked with covenant obligations – of faithfulness to God who had brought them out of Egypt. Moses had even foreseen the possibility of the people being ejected from the land and returning. He said, *"when you and your children return to the Lord your God and obey him with all your heart and with all your soul according to everything I command you today, then the Lord your God will restore your fortunes and have compassion on you and gather you again from all the nations where he scattered you"* (Deut 30:2-3).

The land of Israel was given as a sacred trust, dating back to Genesis 17:8 and Genesis 48:4. It was given for a purpose, not as a possession. The purpose of God for the people of Israel was that they should be his servant through whom he could reveal himself to the nations of the world. This was their inheritance.

68 LISTING THE TRIBES Ezekiel 48

These are the tribes, listed by name . . . Bordering the territory of Judah from east to west will be the portion you are to present as a special gift. It will be 25,000 cubits wide, and its length from east to west will equal one of the tribal portions; the sanctuary will be in the centre of it. The sacred portion you are to offer to the Lord will be 25,000 cubits long and 10,000 cubits wide. This will be the special portion for the priests . . . In the centre of it will be the sanctuary of the Lord. This will be for the consecrated priests . . .

The boundaries of the land had been explained in the previous chapter where it had been stated that the land had to be divided equally between the 12 tribes. Here we have the location of each of the tribal inheritances with the centre of the whole territory being dedicated to the Lord as a holy city. Jerusalem is not named although this may be assumed from the overall layout of the land. The primary intention is to stress the centrality of the presence of the Lord in the land where he is surrounded by the tribes of his people, the family of Abraham and his successors – Isaac and Jacob – the house of Israel.

For Ezekiel the day was now in sight when the exiles would be free to return to the land of their forefathers. This was the day for which he had spent many years preparing the people. They would be re-entering the land to claim their inheritance, but it was essential that God should be in the very centre and heart of the nation. This would show that they had learned from the experience in Babylon that the conditions of the Covenant had to be fulfilled. By putting God in the centre of the nation they would never again despise him by worshipping idols. Their future history would demonstrate this, as none of the postexilic prophets ever charged the nation with idolatry – there were plenty of other sins, but idolatry was never one of them.

Another valuable lesson that the exiles learnt from their sojourn in Babylon was the value of community, of working together and caring for one another. They had learned this in the settlements scattered around Babylon – some of them engaged in agricultural occupations, and others pursued commercial and administrative activities. At the beginning of the exile Jeremiah had urged them to seek the peace and prosperity of Babylon because if it prospered, they too would prosper (Jer 29:7). They undoubtedly prospered, as the record of the freewill offering given for the rebuilding of the temple, when they arrived back in Jerusalem, clearly demonstrated. They gave about 500 kg of gold and 2.9 metric tons of silver (Ezra 2:69).

Ezekiel's vision for the division of the land showed a large area on the outskirts of the city which was to be left for common use, for houses and pastureland. The produce from this land was to be used to feed the workers in the city, and the workforce for the common land would come from all the tribes. Each of the tribes would therefore contribute to the common good – an early form of food banks for those in need.

The final regulation was for the gates of the city to be named after the tribes of Israel. Each of the 12 tribes would have a gate bearing its name which would reinforce the collective sense of belonging and the unity of the nation. There would no longer be a division between the 10 tribes of Israel and the two tribes of Judah and Benjamin. The whole family of Israel would be one people under God. This was always God's intention for his people and it was tragic that it took the disaster of the destruction of both Israel and Judah to produce the exile which was the cradle of the postexilic united nation of Israel. This was something that Jeremiah foretold.

"See, I will bring them from the land of the north and gather them from the ends of the earth . . . They will come with weeping; they will pray as I bring them back . . . He who scattered Israel will gather them and will watch over his flock like a shepherd. For the Lord will ransom Jacob and redeem them . . . I will turn their mourning into gladness; I will give them comfort and joy instead of sorrow . . . The days are coming, declares the Lord, when I will plant the house of Israel and the house of Judah with the offspring of men and of animals. Just as I watched over them to uproot and tear down, and to overthrow, destroy and bring disaster, so I will watch over them to build and to plant" (Jer 31:8-28).

CONCLUSION
THE UNIQUE MESSAGE OF EZEKIEL

Ministry of The Prophets of Israel

Each of the prophets of Israel were men of their day who studied what today we would call the 'signs of the times'. They were watchmen looking at what was happening on the international scene as well as being keen observers of the domestic scene. They not only saw the things that were happening in their day, but they also studied the history of their nation and of those surrounding Israel. They learned to observe social change and social trends. They were what today we would call good sociologists.

Each of the prophets adds to our knowledge of God – of his nature and purposes. Amos speaks of God's 'justice', while Jeremiah stresses the 'covenant' in God's relationships. Ezekiel is known for his revelation of the 'holiness' of God. Holiness is separation from the material world of God's creation, including human beings, the height of his creation. It is God's desire that all human beings should come to know him and to understand his nature and purposes. Towards this end God chose the people of Israel as a vehicle through whom he could reveal himself to the world.

The Covenant

In order to carry out his purposes God created a covenant relationship between himself and his people Israel similar to that of a marriage between a husband and wife. The relationship had to be one of love and trust, loyalty, and integrity. For the guidance of his people Israel God had given the Decalogue and the Torah to Moses for his teaching of the people – the first requirement of which was that the people should have no other God.

Ezekiel's Teaching

Much of the teaching given by Ezekiel was related to the holiness of God and the holiness that he required in his people. They had to be different from the Gentile nations so that God could use them to reveal himself to the world. That difference did not mean that they were superior to the Gentiles, but that they were set apart in order to be the servants of God revealing his nature and purposes. This meant that they had to put God first in the life of the nation – like a light on a mountain.

The people of Israel were intended to be a shining light in the world conveying truth, integrity, honesty, faithfulness and all the values of the kingdom of God. This truth is set out in Ezekiel 5 where God declares his intention of cleansing the city of Jerusalem, burning it with fire, in line with the principle of 'death and resurrection' which lies at the heart of God's creation. He then says, "This is Jerusalem, which I have set in the centre of the nation, with countries all around her" (5:5).

Separation from the World

Ezekiel sees the need for the people of Israel to be holy, separated from the world, so that his presence and his word can be revealed to the nations. He rightly sees that God had to send his people away into exile from the land which they regarded as Yahweh's special dwelling place, so that they could perceive the omnipresence of the God of creation who held the nations in his hands as a drop in a bucket as Isaiah had perceived.

Ezekiel also recognised the need for a redeemed remnant who would go back and rebuild Jerusalem where the presence of God would be established in the centre of the life of the nation. He recognised that the temple which had been desecrated by idolatry had to be destroyed, and also the monarchy, debased by a succession of un-godly Kings, was no longer of value.

Both the destruction of the temple and the monarchy were foreseen by Jeremiah. Ezekiel followed most of his teaching including the establishment of a covenant of peace – but he could not abandon his priestly background and accept the destruction of the priesthood and the temple. The new covenant, as Jeremiah foresaw, would enable everyone to know God for themselves and not to have to rely on a priest. We have to reach the New Testament and the Day of Pentecost before that becomes a reality.

Two Major Concepts

There are two major concepts that come out of the revelation of 'holiness' in Ezekiel's teaching, they are 'Justice' and 'Wrath' both of which are part of the nature of God and are fundamental revelations of truth.

Throughout the Book, Ezekiel uses the phrase "Then they will know that I am God". This is used more than 75 times and occurs more in Ezekiel than in any other place in the Bible. When this is applied to Israel it is an acknowledgement of the constant disobedience of the people of Israel throughout their history. This is referred to by Jeremiah where God says, "*For when I brought your forefathers out of Egypt and spoke to them, I did not just give them commands about burnt offerings and sacrifices, but I gave them this command: Obey me, and I will be your God and you will be my people*" (Jer 7:22-23). Obedience was more important than sacrifices.

Ezekiel was aware of the historic defilement of the land by idolatry and a major objective of his ministry was to ensure there was a change of heart and mind among the exiles until they reached the point where they "loathe themselves" for their sinfulness. It was only when there is true repentance that they could be in a covenant relationship with the holiness of God. He uses the phrase, "They will know that I am God". He is looking forward to the time when the people will come to know God through his redemptive acts, both in forgiving his wayward people and in restoring the covenant relationship that was established at Sinai. In order to do this God himself had to cleanse his people from the defilement of sin. This atonement, made by God, would enable them to have fellowship with the holiness of God.

The Wrath of God

God himself would do the act of cleansing as part of his tender care for his people, just as a shepherd cares for the well-being of his sheep. This reveals something of the tender loving care in the nature of God's relationship with the people of Israel. This love of God is seen even in times of rebuke which gives a new understanding of the term 'wrath' as a mixture of anger, concern, and tender love.

It is like we see in Mary's loving rebuke of the young Jesus when he remained in the temple talking with the rabbis instead of joining the pilgrims returning to Nazareth. His parents had gone a whole day before they discovered his absence then they had to return to Jerusalem. After three days searching for him, he was found in the temple and Mary grumbled, "*Son, why have you treated us like this? Your father and I have been anxiously searching for you*" (Luke 2:48). This was a mixture of anger, anxiety, and tender love, very similar to the 'wrath of God' being poured out upon the people of Israel whom he loved.

This is an important revelation which we find in Ezekiel that shows us part of the nature of God. It also reveals a part of his purposes in restoring the covenant relationship with his people whom he had chosen to be 'a nation of priests', who would be his servant through whom he would reveal his nature and purposes to the Gentile nations.

The Central Role of Jerusalem

Jerusalem had a special part to play within the purposes of God, and it was his intention to use Israel to teach the Gentiles to know him. It is necessary here to return to Ezekiel 5:5-6: "*This is Jerusalem, which I have set in the centre of the nations, with countries all around her. Yet in her wickedness she has rebelled against my laws and decrees more than the nations and countries around her. She has rejected my laws and has not followed my decrees.*"

This statement is followed by charges that the people of Israel had been even more unruly than the nations around them, and they had not even conformed to the standards of the Gentile nations. This was why God was inflicting punishment upon Jerusalem. He would use the city as a warning to the other nations who would see God's wrath in his 'stinging rebuke' of his own people. Even in the destruction of Jerusalem, God would be working out his purposes to reveal himself to the Gentiles which they would see when his covenant people were back in the land.

Judgement and the Covenant People of Israel

In Ezekiel's teaching, justice in the nature of God demanded that punishment should be given to sinful people, including his own chosen people. But punishment was always redemptive – looking for repentance and change in the sinners. Jeremiah was always looking for repentance even when the Babylonians were outside the walls of Jerusalem because he knew that if the people repented and came weeping before God, he had the power to pour out a plague upon the enemy as he had done in the time of Isaiah (Is 37:36).

Ezekiel saw the same loving concern for the people of Jerusalem when the presence of the Lord was leaving the temple and about to leave the city. The glory of the Lord moved from the holy of holies and paused over the east gate, as though God was waiting for a last-minute repentance and change of heart among his people.

Judgement and the Gentile Nations

In connection with God's witness to the Gentile nations Ezekiel uses the phrase, "Then they will know that I am God". The nations that had scoffed at Israel's defeat and said that their God did not have the power to defend them would now see the power of God. They would see his sovereignty displayed in his power over all the nations. Importantly, they would see the nature of God in his justice – punishing the shedding of innocent blood, greed and arrogance as in Isaiah 2:17.

The Grace of God

The grace of God is seen in the tenderness with which he deals with the exiles immediately after the destruction of Jerusalem. He speaks of towns being inhabited and ruins rebuilt in a time of blessing and prosperity. "*No longer will I make you hear the taunts of the nations, and no longer will you suffer the scorn of the peoples*" (36:15).

The free and unmerited grace of God is seen in his action in dealing with the past sins of his people as soon as they repent. He himself carries out the atonement of his covenant people. "*I will sprinkle clean water on you, and you will be clean.*" Then he gives them the promise "*I will give you a new heart and put a new spirit in you*" (36:25-26), which was a messianic promise fulfilled in the life, death, and resurrection of Jesus.

Relevance For Today

The importance of the message of Ezekiel for today lies in the revelation of the unchanging nature and purposes of God. This has to be applied by each generation to their times. It can only be done by those who are part of that generation as Ezekiel had to be part of the company of exiles in Babylon so that he could experience all that they had experienced. It is an essential truth that if we want to communicate the gospel to others we have to begin where they are and bring truth in terms that they can understand.

Ezekiel's revelation of the way God deals with sinful humanity is of permanent value in every generation. So too was his revelation of the nature of God's wrath towards his covenant people and in a different way towards those who have no covenant relationship with him. This shows the different ways in which the gospel has to be applied to different groups – to believers and to non-believers.

It is of particular interest to note the grace of God – his free and totally unmerited grace shown to sinful human beings which is the major characteristic of the justice of God; so skilfully illustrated by Jesus in parables such as the lost son and the employer who went out into the market at different points during the day to hire men, but at the end of the day he paid all the same amount. God's justice is quite different from that of human beings.

Ezekiel's teaching on idolatry which was so detestable to God, has considerable relevance for us today because we certainly do worship 'wood and stone' although in very different forms from the nations around Judah in Ezekiel's day. It is as hard to put our trust in God rather than in our weapons, our wealth, our treaties with other nations or personal friendships as it was for the Jews.

Ezekiel's teaching on 'The Covenant' is relevant today for the disciples of Jesus who are in a New Covenant relationship with God the Father. We constantly break the covenant by failure to honour the obligations of love-relationships – putting God first, others next, and self last. We fail to honour God by witnessing to him in our daily lives and recognising the awesomeness of worshipping him *"acceptably with reverence and awe"* (Heb12:28).